Better Tennis

Better Tennis

JOHN CROOKE

Kaye & Ward

First published in Great Britain by
Kaye & Ward Ltd.
The Windmill Press, Kingswood, Tadworth, Surrey
1984

ISBN 0 7182 1465 X

Printed in Great Britain by
Biddles Ltd.
Guildford and King's Lynn

Contents

About This Book
and The Author

Young, or old, are you keen to start Tennis, or eager to introduce a son, or daughter, to this sport? Are you already a tennis-player of some experience wishing to progress faster and further? If so, this book is for you. WHY?

Because the subject is considered in exactly the way demanded by YOUR situation. Something to help you enjoy yourself successfully on court is on the very first page. Very simply, all the essential information is marshalled under four straightforward headings –
BALL — BAT — BODY — BRAIN
(Racket)
– and there are scores of aids to memory included in the logically presented text and illustrations.

Coaches, too, will find this approach helpful. Not only are technical aspects analysed systematically and numerous challenging practices suggested, but the whole tenor of instruction is closely in line with The Lawn Tennis Association's Coaches' Training syllabus.

The author inaugurated and, for the first four years, directed The Coaches' Training programme for The Professional Tennis Coaches' Association of G.B. and has trained over three thousand coaches operating worldwide. For six further years, as Secretary of The British Association of National Coaches, he was primarily responsible for planning in-service-training for national coaches, team-managers and technical staff, of every British sport.

He was twice British Professional Men's Doubles Champion and coached such players as Gerald Battrick (British Hardcourts Champion and Davis Cup No.1) and the renowned 'JPR', both of these players winning The British 'Junior Wimbledon' title, but he does not dictate how you should play – you choose from what is, often amusingly, suggested, with your decisions being gently guided.

His theme of Ball/Bat/Body/Brain runs like an insistent rhythm throughout the book, moving from elementary advice through to a comprehensive survey of every aspect of a tennis player's progress.

You might think that you are part of your own, or your pupil's, tennis problem. This book could make you most of the solution!

Acknowledgements

The author would especially wish to thank his wife, Betty; Roger Price (Newport), for most of the photography; Alan Sanigar (Plymouth), for most of the drawings; Jean Day, Ann McNamara, David Kilby and Mark Cox, for their encouragement, patience and skilful assistance, without which this book would not have been possible.

The author is also most grateful to Pam Giles, Peter Smowton, Jennifer Blyth-Lewis, Nicola Hall, John Day, Bob Louis and his daughter, Jo, and to Alan Roberts, Ken Rose and Jean Jones, for their help.

Permission to use their photographs has been very kindly given by Adidas, Reginald Blyth-Lewis (Tunbridge Wells), Arthur Cole (Beckenham), Dunlop Sports Co. Ltd., and Roger Hodge (Lympstone), and the consistent support, received over so many years, from John Barrett and Slazengers Ltd. is very gratefully recognised.

The co-operation of The Boughey Gardens Trust (Newport), Woodfield Tennis Club (Shrewsbury) and The Sports Council (Bisham Abbey National Sports Centre and Lilleshall Hall National Sports Centre), in allowing the use of their courts for the illustrations, is greatly appreciated.

The help and backing of The Lawn Tennis Association and The Professional Tennis Coaches' Association of G.B., throughout the author's professional life, has been invaluable, as has the advice and guidance of older (and younger) colleagues, whilst the response from pupils has provided an endless source of knowledge and pleasure.

John Crooke
Shrewsbury March 1984.

Foreword

In the time I have been associated with Tennis I have met many great philosophers on the game and numerous characters within it. But comics are too busy jesting to afford the time to be serious and wise men so busy thinking they soon forget the art of having fun. A good teacher needs a happy blending of both these qualities of knowledge and humour to be able to absorb and inspire his pupils. In this context John Crooke is an outstanding example of a coach with a philosoper's insight into the many facets of the game and an entertainer's talent for attracting and holding his listener's attention. Thus he makes the most efficient use of your time by achieving the maximum response from you.

When I first heard John lecture on Tennis perhaps the most shattering thing was not just how much he was able to teach me, but how much fun it was to listen. He has a knack of opening so many doors in the mind that he really made me feel the draught. It was embarrassing as a fully fledged touring professional to find how much more there was to learn.

Children, especially, need at all times to be shown that the effort they are making to learn will be a productive one. The game must always be projected as a vital and satisfying subject, and the prospect of playing it must appeal. It is no good dangling a carrot if the carrot, on consumption, tastes rotten.

This book will be a stimulating experience for both parent and child, and through it teacher and pupil will find how much pleasure learning Tennis gives them. Which is how it should be.

Winning is always fun, but having fun is more important. This book teaches you how to do both.

MARK COX

1. FIRST THINGS FIRST

Almost certainly by the time you pick up and glance at this book, whatever your age, you will have
(a) Been on court with an opponent, or partner,

or

(b) Watched others play (perhaps on television)

or

(c) Hit against the garage or school wall. Also, you probably played, and will play for a time, with a racket that you happen to have, therefore, what you require in the way of advice now is something that fits that situation on the very first page. Later you may read about racket selection, joining clubs, wider techniques and tactics and scoring, etc., but for now think in terms of

Ball   **Bat (Racket)**   **Body**   **Brain**

Make this your theme and always Ball first.

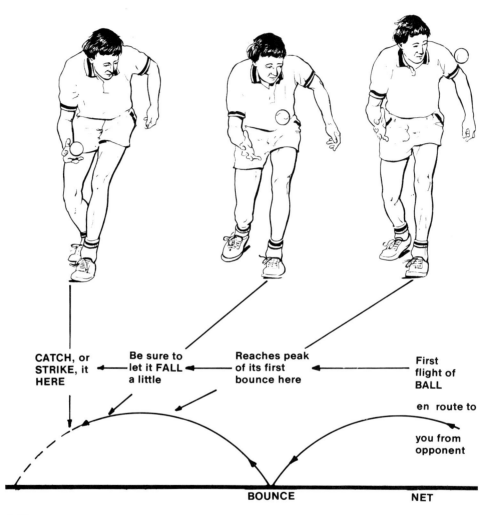

CATCH, or
STRIKE, it
HERE

Be sure to
let it FALL
a little

Reaches peak
of its first
bounce here

First
flight of
BALL

en route to

you from
opponent

BOUNCE

NET

1/1 The Falling Ball

1/2 'Hand-Tennis' close to the net, as here, is a good introductory practice.
The game of 'Short-Tennis' (light, short-handled, plastic bat and 'foam' ball) is, also, helpful for very young beginners.

BALL

Look at illustration 1/1 opposite. Next time on court try to take the ball *after it has reached the peak of its first bounce.*

Whenever you are on court relate to the ball in this way. Simple advice and if you really do that you will progress more quickly.

Ball

See how on forehand and backhand the ball is being played between waist and knee (illustrations 1/3 and 1/4).

11

1/3 Falling ball at thigh height on Forehand Drive.

1/4 Falling ball at thigh height on Backhand Drive.

So, try to read the flight of the ball, predict where it will bounce and meet it at waist height, or a little lower, with racket outstretched. If you manage just that fairly regularly, you are on your way, even if many of your shots go way off the target! Close the book for a moment and try to think what the simple phrase, 'Hit the ball when it is falling towards its second bounce and just lower than the waist,' really helps you to do. Do not cheat, close the book and think!

Right, now check off if your thoughts agreed with this list.

(a) The ball is closely watched with a definite objective in view.

(b) The feet are moved.

(c) The body relates to the ball in nearly the same way each time.

(d) The slightly slower falling-ball fits in comfortably and weightily onto the racket strings as you lift the ball over the net.

(e) There is a little more time to swing your racket and judge its contact with the ball.

12

1/5 Even John McEnroe
regularly takes the falling
ball at thigh height!

1/6 Racket ready to start forward swing on the Forehand.

1/7 Finish of follow through on the Forehand.

1/8 Racket ready to start forward swing on the Backhand.

1/9 Finish of follow through on the Backhand.

BAT (Racket)

Look at the illustrations above and see how the racket, or bat, has swung right through the ball on both forehand and backhand.

So, the simple lesson on use of your racket at first is:
take it well back behind you as soon as you know which side you have to play the ball and then try to swing it right through the ball.

Try to keep the face of the racket firm as you hit the ball. (The face is the strings hitting the ball – note the angle of the face in the illustrations.)

Try a few swings without the ball at all – stand sideways to net (perhaps on one of the lines running down the court under the net). Take your racket right behind you until it is held over the line and the court line runs straight along your racket and both shoulders; hold it there for a moment. Now swing it well out from you at an imaginary ball at waist height (try to be coming slightly upwards as the racket passes the front hip) and swing through, stopping when you are again 'on line' – i.e. shoulders and racket all along the court line but with racket now in front (illustration 1/10).

14

1/10 Train your swing

Stand on edge of platform taking racket back as 'train' (ball) approaches. Sweep it away back down the line with a full swing.

The chapters and illustrations on the forehand and backhand drives give you a detailed guide on this but, for the moment, do not worry too much about the pathway of the swing, just make sure it is not a push, a chop, a flick, a slap, or a jab, but a smooth swing.

BODY

Look again at the illustrations (1/1 - 1/10) – see how the body is sideways – onto the base line of the court and the net as the ball is struck. If, on your first few sessions, you could just master that you would be doing well.

BRAIN

Probably you are on court with a parent, other relative, or friend. Probably you are with someone who is a beginner, or inexperienced player, like you. (Even if you and/or your partner have some experience, these few tips will very likely assist you to practise more purposefully, effectively and, above all, enable you to enjoy what you are doing.)

Think of these – **Concentration**
Control
Co-operation
Competition.

A little later the important reasons why you actually do need to concentrate will be explained, but it is commonsense that a fast-moving ball, a moving opponent, a high net (an all too small court!) and perhaps even a strange racket, all need concentration to achieve

results, so   – **Concentrate**
and at first merely try to   – **Control**
the ball sufficiently well to   – **Co-operate**
with your partner, in order to – **Compete**
later on and see which one is   – **Champion**

Even if, at first, you have to stand very near the net to achieve any success, try to co-operate with your partner in setting up a rally (a few shots in succession) with your partner.

Help!!

The following little plan might help you to progress to a form of game quickly. If you are reading this with virtually no tennis experience, do not worry too much about service, or rules, at this stage, just use yourself, your partner, the ball and rackets and the net and lines, very simply and have fun co-operating and competing. Start very modestly, only making the challenge more ambitious as you progress and gain confidence. Do not be afraid to go back a stage in the **Help** plan if you hit a snag.

16

H Hold the ball.

E Easy underarm throw to your partner.

L Lengthen the practice.

P Play a form of game.

Look at illustrations 1/11 - 1/14 on pages 17, 18 and 19 and see how gradually to increase the difficulty and challenge.

Hold   the ball as high as you can and drop it slightly in front and well to the side of you; after it has bounced and as it is *falling* past your waist, hit it into the netting with a good swing.

Easy   throws, underarm, from you to your partner, or from your partner to you, in order that hitter has an easy opportunity to play a good stroke back for thrower to try to catch.

Lengthen   the practice by thrower and hitter moving back a little and then both of you using rackets and trying to keep a rally going.

Play   a form of game. Co-operate for four shots (two drives each), hitting ball to your partner, then try to compete; attempt to beat your partner, who now becomes your opponent, by placing the ball away from him (her), or hitting faster, lower, or farther away from the net. Maybe, just use one lengthways half of the court as in illustration 1/12, or whole court, 1/13.

1/11a   HELP

Help each other by feeding the ball in progressively more difficult ways. Just ask someone, coach, partner, parent, to drop the ball for you to practise the swing, hitting ball into surround netting. Or drop it for yourself and hit it, or watch a better player do the swing into netting then immediately copy the action.

1/11b HELP

After some practice swinging
to hit ball, into surround netting, move
to more realistic hitting over net, but
keep challenge simple by partner
throwing and you hitting carefully
produced drives for them to catch.

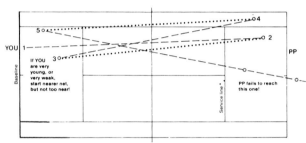

1/12 HELP

The 'L' stage of the helping each
other Feeding Sequence. Just YOU
and your practice-partner (PP) try to
control an easy rally down one
lengthways half of the court. Even five
good shots is very creditable if you
are both beginners, probably all
Forehands at first, but try a few
Backhands!

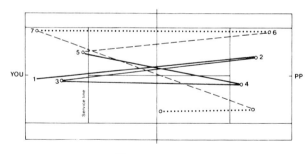

1/13 HELP

The 'P' stage of the helping each
other Feeding sequence.
'PLAY' Actually play AGAINST each
other

The
CO-OPERATING SHOTS are shown
by the continuous lines.
COMPETITIVE SHOTS from you are
broken lines and
COMPETITIVE SHOTS from 'PP' are
dotted lines.
YOU win this one as 'PP' nets the
eighth shot!

CO-OPERATE for four shots, perhaps
trying to place them all beyond the
Service-line, as illustrated, then by
making your practice partner (**PP**) run
wider.
COMPETE Your strokes are the odd
number ones and your
practice-partner has the even ones.

Your shots are broken lines. Partners are dotted lines.

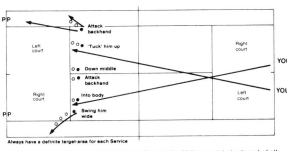

Attack
backhand

Left
court

'Tuck' him up

Right
court

Down middle

Attack
backhand

Right
court

Into body

Left
court

Swing him
wide

Always have a definite target-area for each Service

● indicates bounce of service and o indicates direction in which server is trying to make ball travel.

YOU

YOU

Now you have only to stand in a good position for Service, with 'PP' in a good Receiving position and you could play a very elementary game, perhaps even serving underarm at first. Right from the start try to have a definite target point for your service in right and left courts. Start the game in the right court, across to Receiver in his right court. Service must land in service court. All other shots must be inside Singles, or Doubles, courts according to how many are playing. See also Figure *5/1* PP's position will vary with age and standard – experiment!

Practice and practices

The next few chapters will take you further into stroke production and into better tennis, but at least you have made a sound start. Interesting practice and forms of match-play are most important to your progress and after each chapter you will find details of functional practices, all very simple, active and purposeful, but, above all, enjoyable.

A quarter-of-an-hour enjoying yourself, but not fooling on court, will help your tennis advance far more than hours of dull routine or careless play. To become really sound in strokes you will need to work a little at your game and drive yourself as well as the ball, but, even when working at your game, you should be playing it! Play it, but not at it!

By all means break off trying to get the swing right and play a few points, or games; certainly finish your service practice by hammering a few volleys at your opponent. Use this book as a friend who wants to help, but remember you are the one who does the learning and you do not have to be taught in order to learn! Who actually taught you to lick ice-cream? You experimented; do that with your tennis. If you had a train, bus, or plane, to catch and, having just packed your case to the brim, suddenly you found a vital item outside the overfull case, what would you do? You might unpack it completely, re-arrange carefully to include the vital item, or you might

19

just quickly pull out something not too important and hurriedly cram in the missing item. Your tennis strokes are like your case; this book might indicate that there is a vital item missing. Now it will depend upon the sort of person you are and the amount of time that you have available which way you repack. The choice is yours – slow careful building of your all-round game, or a quick attempt to strengthen a few of the real weaknesses. Either way you could become a champion; either way you could enjoy getting what you actually achieve on court a little nearer what you are capable of achieving. These few practices might help.

Elementary driving practices

  (i) Try to co-operate with your partner as before but, this time, set a target of at least eight consecutive shots without either of you missing the ball.

 (ii) Try eight shots again and, if you succeed, whatever higher number you reach, make the target for the very next rally, nine shots without a mistake. If you fail to reach nine, go back to eight again, but if you succeed, and reach nine, or more, try ten on the next rally and so on.

(iii) Try practice (ii) as explained but, as soon as you reach your target figure, try to *end* the rally quickly by changing from co-operating with your partner and start competing against him or her as your opponent!

(iv) Stand well back in the court now and try to keep a rally of at least six shots going, all of which land between the service-line (that is the one running across the court about half-way) and the baseline (the line right at the back of the court). (See illustration 1/12).

 (v) Stand by the 'tramlines' (the lines running like railway tracks right down the court) and see how many shots you are able actually to hit into these 'tramlines'. Just three in succession would be excellent if you are both beginners, but perhaps try for ten landing in the tramlines, in a rally that includes shots landing a little to the side of either line. (Of course, you must start counting from one again when the ball is missed, goes too wide, or in the net!).

20

B

C

1/15   Reading the Signals

How well do you **READ** the signals available in these figures?

The ball is the main signal for you, giving vital information, but the opponent's racket movement and angles and the body position of the opponent and even the score, all help you to predict what is highly likely to happen in any situation.

No ball is visible here in these four shots yet you should be able to tell which two shots have slice on them, which two are top-spin, which two went diagonally across the court and which two were coming at you straight down the line. Answers below, but try first!

It will not take acute powers of observation to see that the one player is wearing a track-suit here and occasionally in other illustrations of practice situations. Never be fool'hardy' and show how you 'brave' the cold! Warm up sensibly and, in cold, damp, weather, wear warm, but un-restricting, clothing, at least in the knock-up. A torn muscle takes longer to heal than damaged pride!

B – Sliced drive straight down the line.
A – Sliced drive diagonally across court.
D – Top-spin straight down the line.
C – Top-spin cross-court drive.

2. THE FOREHAND DRIVE

BALL

Look at the photographs on pages 24 and 25 and notice how the player is taking the ball level with the thigh and in a position that allows a full, free, swing – not too close or cramped.

BRAIN

In order to do this regularly and well, you must try, like a general in battle, to guess accurately where the enemy attack is directed! Read the signals! Gradually you will remember from previous shots from your opponent, or rallies with your partner, that certain things are most likely to happen. If you have just hit a particularly poor, weak, shot to your opponent, then it is likely to come back to you in a way that is rather awkward for you; possibly travelling fast and probably into a space left unguarded by you.

Signals

Try to see how strongly your opponent's racket appears to be travelling in its swing – this will tell you a little about the strength and weight of shot you will soon be attempting to meet. If the opponent looks well balanced then the shot might be hit very firmly. If you hear and see a mis-hit, poorly timed shot, be ready for a shorter ball. Does the opponent's body position give you a clue as to the direction the ball might go. Look back at the illustrations on page 21. You will pick up some tips on direction there.

Those photographs (late in the stroke, after the ball has disappeared) are to alert you to the wealth of information there to be seen. You should not need such signals to tell you what has happened after your opponent has hit the ball, but concentrate your detective powers earlier and earlier in your opponent's build-up, picking up vital clues. You will not be Sherlock Holmes straightaway! Start as an 'Inspector', a close inspector of all that is happening; recall what has happened previously and outdo Sherlock Holmes by predicting what will happen!

BALL

Now the ball itself. Does it go up high off the opponent's racket – if so it might be travelling quite slowly but it also might be a very long shot from which you have hurriedly to move back. Does it seem to be spinning very much? Try to predict where it will bounce and do not be close to that bounce if you possibly can avoid it, otherwise your shot will have to be very hurried. Judge your footwork to be nearer the second bounce (illustration 1/1) but, of course, hit it before that second bounce! You cannot actually watch the ball right on to the racket, but try to!

BAT AND BODY

The illustrations and captions on the next two pages give the main points on how to use your racket and how to place your body and the following pages tell you more about forehand drives and how to practise them.

BOOKS

A surprising addition to our four 'B's, but important. Helping your game through a book compels an author to be 'authoritative', whereas a wise coach follows a freer approach. To become a tennis-star does not demand slavish imitation of strokes shown. Highlighted overleaf is a 'neutral' forehand (no excessive spin, or angles, etc.). Value it as a broad guide, remembering that many great forehands are played more 'square-on' to net and that your stroke will subtly differ each time owing to many variables. The vital thing on 'every stroke in the book' is to 'use' each ball effectively.

2/1 The Forehand Drive

**BAT
(Racket)**
The path
and pace
of the
swing

Position of Readiness

Racket held comfortably across front of body; pointing slightly towards opponent but be natural!

Backswing

Racket has moved slightly upwards in backswing and loops down into forward swing

BODY
Footwork
and balance

Behind baseline; alert relaxed; springily balanced on both feet.

Body has turned sideways; pivot (sometimes even a step and pivot) on right foot then step forward and slightly across with left foot.

24

No two players perform their strokes in the same way, but all keep to certain principles Merely observe these and try to make your shots simple and natural.

Hitting Point

Racket held firmly swings up at ball, well out from body, striking ball opposite leading hip, or thigh.

Follow-Through

Racket swings on through ball, lifting it over net to high finish.

Weight comes forward from right foot onto left, knees slightly bent.

Body has helped shot by pivoting slightly; then recovery quickly for next shot.

2/2 The Forehand Drive

BAT (RACKET)	Swing	PATH	Using a 'loop' smooths backwards movement	into forward movement,
		PACE	Early backswing enables	sustained preparation on slower balls
	Face	WRIST	Slightly 'cocked' in	take back, coming into line
		GRIP	Shake hands with palm behind	racket handle;

FOLLOW EACH SUB-DIVIDED LINE RIGHT ACROSS BOTH PAGES

BODY	Footwork	POSITION	Move early as you might have	to run across court
		STANCE	Prepare on the right foot	stepping in with
	Balance	WEIGHT	Try to 'gather'	the weight over the right
		CONTROL	By keeping legs 'springy'	and 'sinking' over bent knees

racket slightly below ball	just before impact,	and lifting firmly	through.
and building up strong rush	of acceleration into	and through the	faster ones.
with the arm as racket swings	forward to ball, face of racket	kept steady throughout	'guaranteeing' ball's direction
firmly gripped just before	and thus steadying face on impact	and right through	to end of stroke.

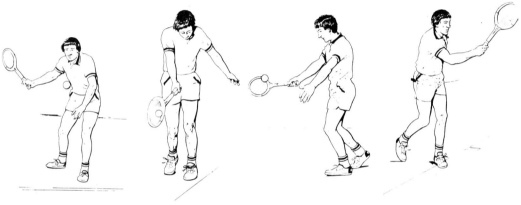

whilst the racket swing is building up;	try to arrive at	a point alongside	the ball's flight.
the left foot	as the ball is struck;	the right foot being	nearly off ground in follow-through
foot, transferring it onto left	as ball is struck; this gives length and power as you are	hitting with the body	as well as arm and racket.
hugging ground with feet,	the contact with ball is balanced	and firm and body rises up	to finish helping lift ball deep to opponent's court.

Forehand drive – further points

The illustrations and captions on pages 24 to 27 give you most of the information you need to go out and practise effectively but here are a few more tips to round off this stroke.

Ball

This absolutely governs you in two ways once service has been played because,

   (i) Your opponent's shot to you dictates to what point you have to move in order to make contact at all –

and –

  (ii) Your sole intention is not to perform a glorious ballet-like movement of beauty, but to ensure that the ball goes back to your opponent's court in the most attacking way possible in any given situation. It might only be a question of saving a point by somehow clearing the net, or you might be going for an outright winner but the ball is the thing –

predict it

relate to it

'feel it'

use it.

BAT (Racket)

The vital principles of use of the racket on any stroke are

(a) An efficient grip.

(b) A good pathway for the swing.

(c) Careful timing of the swing.

(d) Firm, sensitive, control of the racket-face.

Grip

This is so important it has a chapter all on its own comparing all grips and advising their uses (pages 57-59).

Swing – the path of it.

Backswing – Why a shallow loop in the illustrations?

28

Because –

(a) A smoother movement results from no stopping of the racket as it changes from going backwards to coming forwards.

(b) Relating to oncoming ball is easier; fast ball/fast loop back; slow ball/ slow sustained loop back.

(c) It assists dealing with unexpected heights of ball, a low 'shooter', or a sudden high 'sit-up'.

Take the swing back early (making certain the hand as well as the racket head goes well back behind the body) and make a full sweep of arm and racket not a wristy flick.

Forward swing – the vital section

Although the preparatory backswing is important, the forward swing is even more crucial to the success of your stroke. It should come up at the ball a little, so, try to get the racket's 'loop' completed well before hitting the ball and then swing firmly through the ball well out from the body, finishing quite high, as the ball usually has to go a long way to be effective. Murmur to youself, 'press', and, 'get that ball away', as you make contact to ensure a good firm grip on impact and the feeling of the positive forward swing.

Pace (Backswing)

The success of your stroke will also depend very heavily on the pace of your swing. Take the racket back too late and a hurried swing will be produced, so as a general guide, get the racket back as early as possible and it is better to be too soon than too late! However, try to get it just right! See chart on pages 112 and 113.

Pace (Forward swing)

This will depend upon how hard you intend to hit the shot and whether you plan applying considerable spin, or want an especially sharp angle, etc.

Assuming, for the moment, that you want a mildly lifted straight drive to the opponent's baseline, build up the pace of your swing early so that the maximum racket head speed is just before you hit the ball. Remember, too, you do not always want to hit the ball as hard as your strength and technique will possibly permit, although this is what some inexperienced players always seem to try to be doing. Variation of pace can upset an opponent's rhythm and win points for you anyway and sometimes, if an opponent has hit hard to you, use the controlled almost 'brakes-on' pace of your forward swing to take the pace *off* the ball and ensure returning it into court. Finally, a really super swing a fraction of a second too late is probably not as effective as a reasonable swing on time! It can look pretty, but it has to be effective!

2/3b These fairly simple exercises help you to get the 'feel' of the **BALL** on the **RACKET (BAT.)** and show again the various racket angles –

"OPEN"   "CLOSED"   "VERTICAL"

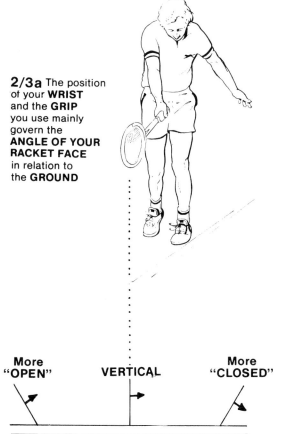

2/3a The position of your **WRIST** and the **GRIP** you use mainly govern the **ANGLE OF YOUR RACKET FACE** in relation to the **GROUND**

More **"OPEN"**   VERTICAL   More **"CLOSED"**

Left-handed Ann, on the left, is keeping a ball bouncing in the air and her racket-face is 'wide-open' as she attempts a hundred consecutive hits. Note how closely all are watching the ball.

John, in the centre, using a slight 'brushing' action across the top of the ball, is controlling the downwards spinning bounce, the racket-face being 'very closed'.

On the right, David is doing a more challenging exercise, bouncing the ball downwards with the edge of a racket that is 'vertical' to the ground. You could try this same exercise upwards, too.

30

Racket-face control

The racket face in tennis coaching terms means the strings of the racket and the angle at which they are presented to the ball. The main points here are grip and wrist position. We know already that the firmer the racket is held the less the wrist will flick about. Look at the racket face angles in illustration 2/3 and remember these main points when you are endeavouring to improve your forehand drive control:

(a) The racket face should be almost vertical to the ground as a basic position.

(b) For dealing with very low bouncing balls coming towards you, you should 'open' the racket face a little, i.e. let the strings open up to the sky slightly, so that the ball is kept out of the net.

(c) If you have a very fast ball to deal with, keep the racket face very firm indeed by gripping tightly and if the ball is also high bouncing and fast, perhaps just 'close' (opposite to open!) the racket face as you follow-through. Experiment how much you need to 'close' in order to keep such balls in court.

BODY

Obviously you will usually not be starting from a position of readiness. You will often be running back from a previous shot. However, if you and a practice-partner have a court all to yourself, you should commence the rally in a good 'ready-position', a foot, or two, behind the centre of your baseline (illustration 2/1). When you are in a game and returning the service, then you stand as indicated in illustration 8/5. After you have played the shot, in a singles practice, or match, do one of these four things:

(a) Try to get back to a central 'ready-position'.

(b) If you anticipate the ball coming back near the side that you are, adjust your position a little, perhaps slightly back towards, or over, the baseline, and be ready for it.

(c) If you think the ball will go to a spot on the court, well away from you, prepare to go to a point a *little behind* that spot by the shortest route.

(d) If you have been pulled near to the net, perhaps inside the service-courts, in order to play the ball, then afterwards immediately, move nearer to the centre of the net, slightly towards the side of your court where you have directed the shot.

Body really means:

(a) Footwork getting to the ball (Preparation).
(b) Footwork playing the ball (Execution).
(c) Balance (Control and power).
(d) Height of body in relation to ball (Adjustment).

Footwork

Footwork in any game is not like dancing – although dancing might help. You cannot have a series of steps all planned out for you for various shots. You keep springily on the balls of your feet, you keep alert and you get there (wherever you are going) as quickly as you can! It is the brain deciding exactly where to go that is crucial to your success; and then your feet in any way comfortable to you, have to take you precisely there and precisely at the right time! Here are general points that suit everybody whether their body is tall and thin, short and thin, or rather more weighty (short or tall).

Footwork (Preparation)

Get a partner to throw a few balls to right and left of you, short and long. You will find instinctively as in illustration 2/4 that if your partner throws a ball to *your right* (as you face the net) and your brain predicts that you will have to play that ball at a point level with your starting position, or at some point farther from the net than your starting position (i.e. behind you and involving a move back) you will start off with a *right* foot movement. You check it! If, however, the ball, again predicted by your brain as likely to be played by you at a point level with you, or behind you, is to your *left*, you will commence with a *left* foot movement. But, should you intend taking the ball to the right and nearer the net than your starting position, what do you find yourself doing? Almost invariably it will be the *left* foot that comes across to start you off. Similarly the right foot will come across if you predict a hitting point to your left and to the front of where you start. A little

32

confusing, but very important. Look at illustration 2/4 and go over it again. From the way your partner throws and the way you 'read' the ball coming towards you, really 'perceive' the point where your paths must meet! Immediately start off in that direction. Long strides crossing normally if you have a long way to run, but shorter strides and possibly skipping, sliding, movements not crossing feet when close to the ball for better balance, although you might have to take one long final stride into the stroke – especially if it is much farther away than you thought likely. If it is closer than you expected you might have to alter your balance and racket swing a little, because however you are positioned the vital point is:

the ball must go back

not

how good you look even if you fall over!

2/4 When ball has to be **Contacted** to player's **Right** – forehand side – at these four different points, indicated by the ball-box, or ball-baskets, note how backwards and sideways movements commence with the *right* foot, whilst forward movements start with *left* foot. (Exactly opposite would be applicable to similar movements to player's **Left** – backhand side).

Footwork (Execution)
Ideally you should stand as if both feet had their toes on the edge of a station platform with, for a right-hander's forehand, the left foot nearer the train coming in from the left! Study again illustration 1/10 on page 15. Your aim is to signal to the driver with a fully stretched flat racket face held like a barrier at right angles to platform high over the tracks. Why?
(a) Free full racket-swing possible.
(b) Weight helps not hinders stroke.
(c) Easier to reach a wide ball and still be balanced.

   However, you cannot always achieve this and the type of stroke attempted might not require this position. Bear it firmly in mind that you cannot play a very successful stroke absolutely square on to the net but as you see in the examples (2/5) you often only need, or have time and space, to turn the upper body, so the 'angle of sidewaysness' will depend upon these factors.
(a) The shot you are attempting (heavy slice down on the ball, or severe top-spin – like Borg – would be helped by a more open – more square on to net – stance.
(b) Where you were on court, where the ball had come from and to where you wanted to hit it.
(c) How much time you had.
(d) If you anticipated that you would have to return very fast back across the court to cover a gap, you would obviously not want to turn so severely sideways in the opposite direction first!

   The golden advice to bear in mind is, you might not always 'put your left foot across' but try during the stroke 'to transfer your weight at least partially on to it', which leads us on to balance.
Balance (Control and power)
In order to get an effective forehand drive you will see the best players transferring their weight smoothly and easily from the rear-foot (the right) onto leading foot (left) as they execute the stroke. Sometimes their left foot will only be just nearer the net than their right; sometimes definitely nearer

the net though not 'across' very much. However, of course, very often it is actually put across so that the body is very distinctly as a whole sideways on to the net as the crucial swing of the stroke is performed. Remember, even if the *feet* are not actually in a full sideways position, the top of the body from knees slightly, and from waist more fully, is rotated as the swing is made, thus, your body is adding power to the swing, without loss of control.

2/5 Awkward Customers!

These strokes look awkward and are awkward! Often you do not have enough time to turn sideways to the net, so, even on difficult, fast, high, balls try to do three things:-
1) Turn upper body a little
2) Get weight 'into' stroke if possible
3) Keep racket-face firm.

**Remember,
it is not where your feet are,
or how you look ...**

**... it is where the ball goes
that really counts!**

Body Height (Adjustment)

One of the oldest sayings in tennis is bend your knees – you rarely hear 'stretch' your knees! Try to think of your knees having three main tasks to perform:

(a) They are your shock absorbers, so that the stroke is smooth.

(b) They are your springs, so that you are quick off the mark and quick in recovery.

(c) They are your height adjusters.

Your knees should always be bent a little during general play and movement anyway, but, of course, they must be well bent for low balls, so that the swing does not become a scoop. You must be ready to bend them quickly if a ball shoots suddenly much lower than expected and occasionally you must straighten them rapidly to get up almost on tip-toe for a ball coming past you higher than anticipated.

BRAIN

Obviously your body has to deal with the stroke, but your brain is nevertheless the more important unit. It is your attitude that is vital in perceiving (judging) the situation and selecting a response (stroke) that will ensure that the ball goes into court effectively. More about this later but concentrate and really will the ball back into court; it will not just go there on its own! Try to plan your returns, not with this scale in mind or you would never be in time for the ball anyway, but with this as your overall guide always:

(a) The ball must go in to court to be of any use to you at all.

(b) It must restrict the choices open to your opponent for his next shot; perhaps ensure that he has to play from far back in his court, perhaps make him play a backhand, etc.

(c) It should put real pressure upon the opponent if possible.

(d) It must take any opportunity there is of an outright winner into an unguarded space.

Concentration is dealt with later so you will read why. For now just be sure to concentrate. The following practices might help:

Practices (Forehand drive)
These follow up and add to those on pages 19 and 20, which should also regularly be used.

(i) If both of you are right-handers, stand just behind the centre of the baseline and hit cross-court to each other's forehands, trying to place the ball beyond the service-line and as near the side-line as you safely can. (With a left-hander and right-hander doing this practice one would be hitting backhands).

(ii) Try a similar practice as (i) but see how many hard, *low*, shots you can both hit without one of you having to step over the baseline to reach the ball.

(iii) You and your practice-partner who is now your 'opponent' start a singles rally, either over the full court, or just down one long half (between the centre of the court and the tram-lines) and just see who wins the point. We will say that you do. You now start off another rally and this time you must win before the rally reaches ten shots. If your opponent manages to keep the rally going beyond ten, you have lost; or obviously you have lost if your opponent actually wins the point inside ten. However, we will again say you have won, so, now, on the next rally you must win the point within nine shots and so on. As soon as the player merely trying to survive a particular number of shots does so or wins the point anyway, the roles change over. You might get the rally survival number down to five, then on the next rally you put the fourth shot in the net. Your partner now has to try to beat you in ten shots, then nine and so on. If you survive the number of shots to be played, or win the point in any way, you take over as the attacker again. This encourages a sensible balance between aggressive, adventurous, play and safe, consistent, control.

Summary

Before we move on to backhand let us sum up so far.

(a) *Early understanding.* If you have easy, well-developed ball-sense, you will soon feel at home on court; if you are not so gifted, familiarise yourself with a ball's movement by throwing and catching, bouncing on the racket, etc. (see pages 10, 11, 17, 18 and 30). Start by standing a comfortable distance from the net and then after a few minutes stop and think. Did every ball seem to need a quick lunge and step forward, or did nearly every ball seem to push you back towards the surround netting? If you always had to stretch forward, move your starting position nearer the net, but however young, or weak do not start nearer the net than the service-line, see illustration 1/12. If you had to run back each time, then start farther from the net, possibly in the best ready-position of all, just behind the baseline. Now you are beginnning to be aware of the court.

(b) *Early development.* Relate to the ball so that it is just falling past the waist, or a little lower, as you swing the racket through at it, well out from your body. Control the face of the racket by a firm shake-hands grip and very little wrist movement. Keep springily on the balls of your feet and mentally on your toes! Get at least partially sideways on to the net to play your stroke. Now you are aware of the ball's movement and the timing of racket and body swing to meet it successfully.

2/6 The High 'C's

**CONCENTRATION
CONTROL
CO-OPERATION
COMPETITION
CHAMPION**

38

CONCENTRATION   CONTROL

(c) *Early tactics*. You usually want the ball to go a fairly long way, so lift it over the net and aim to have the highest point of the ball's flight away from you in the air over your opponent's service-line (see illustration 1/12). Remember the ball has to go over the net and into court for you to survive, let alone win! Now you are aware of your opponent.

(d) **Early memory joggers   A B C**
The three 'A's
Aim   **Alertness**   **Accuracy**

The four 'B's
Ball   **Bat (Racket)**   **Body**   **Brain**

The five 'C's
Concentration Control   Co-Operation Competition 'Champion'

These first two chapters have seen a very lengthy examination of the early requirements for success on court but you now have the vital points in mind. These will be important in the later chapters as so much of the developing advice for you is by way of comparison with this early information and is marshalled under similar headings.

CO-OPERATION   **COMPETITION**   **CHAMPION**

Ball, Bat, Body and **Brain** are important whether one, or two-hands, are used on the backhand, as Jo Louis, one of Britain's leading international junior players and champions, shows here. The maxi-size head of the racket gives a larger 'sweet-spot' on the strings and allows a bigger margin for error.

Jo is taking great care to coax this backhand drive back into court with a firm slice.

Notice the strong close-handed grip, the straight arms and the body weight forward.

3. Backhand Drive

BRAIN

There is a very good reason for starting with brain in this chapter. Discovery is the best way of learning something. Think it out, literally go out and experiment. Do just that with the backhand. You now know quite an amount about forehand; the list below will help you compare the two strokes, so go from the known to the unknown via these headings:

(a) *Ball* – would it be correct to play the falling-ball just about thigh height as with the forehand, or is it different?

(b) *Bat (Racket)* – is the swing of the racket similar to forehand, or different?

(c) *Body* – does the body turn as much, or more, on the backhand? How does the body connect with the racket, via the same grip as forehand, or differently?

(d) *Brain* – what other actions in life do you automatically perform in a backhand-way? Who is your favourite player? How old are you? Does your racket feel very heavy?

Real competitors will try out this little project before turning the page; at the very least the thinking will help you but why not experiment, lawns, or garage doors, usually available! Only then look overleaf and at the illustrations in this chapter.

3/1 The Backhand Drive

**BAT
(Racket)**
The path
and pace
of the
swing

Position of Readiness

If as you return to this position you expect a Backhand prepare for a grip change

Backswing

Racket hand and racket head taken well behind body and slightly below ball

BODY
Footwork
and balance

Do not keep favouring a point on court that tells your opponent you do not like Backhands! Get to the middle.

See how body has turned extra far, weight already fully on leading foot

**Comparison
with
Forehand**

Exactly the same but left hand will help racket take back

More turn; weight on front foot earlier, which allows

42

Hitting Point

Lift the racket into the ball. Note the firm face of racket

Follow-Through

Stay with the ball to ensure length and direction

Weight driving up into stroke as knee straightens

Body mainly on front foot ready to return quickly for next shot

pivot round leading foot instead of transferring weight

Similar to Forehand

43

3/2 The Backhand Drive

BAT (RACKET)	Swing	PATH	Very shallow	loop back
		PACE	Early takeback	building up pace
	Face	WRIST	As firm as grip,	locking straight
		GRIP	Hand comes	more on top

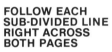

FOLLOW EACH SUB-DIVIDED LINE RIGHT ACROSS BOTH PAGES

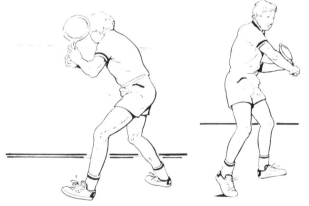

BODY	Footwork	POSITION	Feet moved quickly	to point well away
		STANCE	Both feet as soon as possible on lines	parallel to net, advancing
	Balance	WEIGHT	Attempt to get weight	well over right foot
		CONTROL	Sink into slicing type	of shot to control

below ball;	arm straight well out from	body and lifting ball	high and deep to opponent's baseline
as pivot occurs;	long full flourish	as if drawing	a sword.
with arm, for full	drive with slight top-spin 'roll',	or cocking back to slice	speed off a faster ball
of racket handle	to keep face firm on impact	and through to	end of stroke.

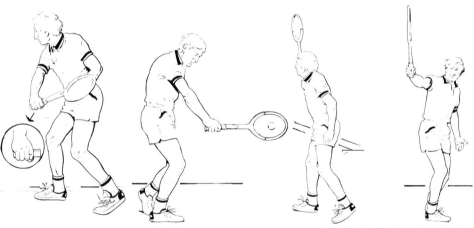

from bounce of ball	taking body completely sideways on	to net and then	recovering back to centre of court.
right foot across and nearer net	to give sound base	for body pivot	into lifted shot.
with bent knee;	pivot hips and lift from	knee so that a 'swing door'	sweeps ball strongly away
faster awkward shots at you	and keep head steady eyes	on ball well after impact	to ensure security of return.

BALL

As you see in illustration 3/1 the ball is taken when it is falling towards its second bounce, almost identically with the ideal hitting point on forehand drive, contact being made about thigh height, possibly regularly just a little lower on backhand, compared with forehand. Especially important is to get the hitting point well clear of the body, perhaps slightly nearer to the net than the point where the leading foot is placed, i.e., well out to the side and to the front of the body itself.

BAT (RACKET)

A swing – it must be. Altered a little from forehand in that you should help it back with the free hand; that certainly will limit the loop; it becomes a more compressed loop, almost a straight take back but try to imagine that your racket-hand (the right for our purposes) goes far enough back to be able to dip into your left (skirt/shorts) pocket. Only then will you know that the racket has gone back far enough. The arm is bent in the take back but straightens very early in the forward swing. Try to hit a full, smooth straight arm swing right through the ball, with plenty of lift, not a nervous chop, or push, down the back of the ball from close to you. Look at the illustrations (4/1 and 4/2) and especially notice the grip change. In fact this is such an important item it has a section all on its own.

BODY

Quite a difference here. The racket is 'attached' to the 'front' of the body on backhand, whereas on the forehand as you turned sideways on to the net the racket was attached at the back of the body, so just a slight turn gives plenty of swinging space on the forehand. Now on the backhand you have to make swinging space by turning well away from the net. Not quite backwards to it, but try to get the right foot well across as in illustrations 3/1 and 3/2. Because of this change there is a difference, too, in weight transference, the weight goes in earlier on a backhand, the whole of the forward swing being played on a pivoting action based on the right (leading) foot.

46

BRAIN

You probably think your opponent has a weaker backhand than forehand; he probably thinks you have, too! So, what a surprise if he suddenly receives a firm, confident, shot from you on this wing! Certainly, if you were asked to push a friend's car and you stayed facing the direction of the push, you would, for sure, use your palms towards the car's surface. That tells us that forehand type movements are pretty strong ones. However, if a friend asked you to throw a book towards him, or if you threw a quoit, or a ring at a fairground, you would very definitely do it in a backhand manner. An indication that natural control and accuracy is a feature of backhand actions – you deal cards backhanded, too. Why should this stroke therefore, be so often so feared? If your favourite tennis star is a double-handed backhand player, or if you feel your stroke is weak because you are very young and/or the racket seems too heavy, by all means put your free-hand on the racket to help and there is a special page on double-handed play in this chapter later. For the moment we will assume just one hand (the right as regularly in this book) is on the racket. Study the illustrations carefully and then let us go through the Ball, Bat, Body, Brain, sequence section by section for the backhand ground-stroke.

BALL

Read the signals. Do you think your opponent might try to slip it across to your backhand this time? As soon as you have picked up the direction, which should be literally in the first few feet of the ball's flight after leaving the opponent's racket, you should be predicting the *likely end of the ball's first flight,* i.e., where will it first bounce? Now, whatever else you do, avoid being anywhere near that actual spot! Think of it as a bomb, that will burst quickly at you. You must be in the broad direction of the ball or you will not reach it, but generally inexperienced players are drawn towards this first bounce as if it were a magnet and get too close, both to the 'line' of the ball across court and the 'length' of it down the court.

Read the flight and try to decide where the second bounce would be.

Remember you are going to hit it a little before the second bounce at about thigh, or knee, height. (In fact a strange practice would help your stroke in the early stages. Allow the ball actually to bounce twice and, having run well back from it, step forwards, bend very low, and lift it over the net with your racket swinging upwards.) When you are playing backhands generally, remember this advice about not being too cramped and close to the ball's line of flight or its bounce.

Follow-up points on backhand drive and practices

As earlier with the forehand the following pages examine under the now familiar headings Bat (Racket) and Body movements necessary in backhand drives and compare them with what you already know on forehand.

BAT (RACKET)

The main aim is to make your backhand side at least as strong as the forehand wing; so many players merely try to dig down with the racket and push the ball weakly back hoping for a forehand next time! Read this and move from that group of players to those who drive up through their backhands.

Path (Forward swing)

With arm straight and racket head well out from body lift firmly up through the ball, the long edge of the racket head nearly parallel to ground as you strike the ball. Remember, your racket head should be like the firm outer edge of a swing-door, your body being its central pillar.

Pace

It does not matter how far your racket travels, what matters is the speed of the racket head hitting the ball but a good, long, early, sustained build-up of pace, especially for younger inexperienced players, makes power plus *control* easier. Swing right on through the ball **but try** to reach the top speed of your swing fractionally before hitting the ball.

Racket-face control

It must be firm on impact. (Look at grip, Chapter four); a slight change of

48

3/3 Beginners should keep wrist locked on most drives, but, with experience, the wrist may be used, as here, to take pace off and control an awkward ball that 'nearly got away'!

3/4 Good contact of feet with ground directly influences the degree of control and power of a stroke, but, as here, it is possible, even when 'airborne', to keep weight 'forward' into the stroke. Opponent's severe shot has driven player well beyond the baseline, but the firm, solid, power of this backhand drive is still very obvious.

3/5 "Wait for it?". Not always! Get in early and attack short length balls from an opponent. Note how the left hand supports the racket's backswing, how closely ball is watched and how strong the good backhand grip looks.

grip for backhand helps this control and you use your wrist for extra subtlety; look at illustration 3/3. You might want top-spin or back-spin depending upon the tactical situation, so alter your wrist position 'to open, or to close' the racket face, but remember you could still *lift* strongly and firmly even if applying a little defensive back-spin.

BODY

Footwork (Preparation)

Use your feet to ensure that vital body turn and to give enough sheer space for a full shot.

Footwork (Execution)

Front foot still and parallel to net as shot made. Finish the stroke completely, then quickly back to cover the next danger area.

49

Balance (Control and power)

Weight must go in early onto the front foot (right foot/right-handers) and the body pivot is the engine-room for your power. Keep head steady and even in an emergency situation, driven backwards see how player in illustration 3/4 has still not fallen away from the stroke. Note in 3/5 the weight obviously coming forward in to a shorter ball.

Body (Height adjustment)

You can rarely get too low! Really bend your knees, it is such a great help in balancing yourself getting up awkward balls, lifting strongly on easier ones and adjusting height in emergencies.

BRAIN

An average ball to deal with? Get into position quickly and try to embarrass him a little by a full length powerfully hit stroke, possibly across court to his backhand! A difficult ball rushes towards you? Decide to play safe and slice the racket down the short-cut on the ball, allowing the fierce pace to waste itself against your more open racket face; perhaps try to float your return deep. A very easy ball drops your way? Confidently sweep it away for a top-spin winner, or angle your racket to give your opponent a wickedly heavy slice that shoots at him like braked wheels skidding on a wet road! Try these tactics and these practices and lose any worries you had about backhands!

3/6 **"LOW AND BEHOLD!"**
A very low ball on the Forehand, or Backhand drive is often even more difficult than a very high one. Copy the player here who is –
1 Bending well down on the right knee
2 Keeping arm straight and only dropping racket head just enough to get under ball
3 Opening the racket-face a little, by turning the wrist slightly
Try to think and act like a golfer playing a very important shot out of a shallow bunker quite close to the green!

50

Practices especially for the backhand ground-stroke (drive).

(i) If you really have difficulty on the backhand try these very simple practices first. Stand by the netting (sideways on and near to), throw a ball up (or ask someone to drop it for you) well out from you and swing your racket in a firmly lifted backhand stroke, driving the ball into the netting; keep your racket face nearly parallel to the netting throughout stroke, a very important point. You will remember that the second 'feeding-stage' in 'HELP' involved a partner throwing to you. Challenge yourself and your partner in these two ways. Your partner (standing just on the far side of the net from you) throws a ball carefully placed so that you are able to meet it well to the side of you, a little forward of the front foot and fairly low in its second flight; you with your backhand drive try to lift a catch to your partner. See how many in succession you can do. Then decide upon a small 'goal' or a 'target' area – any space about half the width of the court, or even a third of its width; use the court lines, or boxes, etc. Your partner again throws an easy ball and you try to put it into the target area past your partner. A point to you if you succeed, or if you make him drop the ball; a point to your partner if you hit the ball in the net, or outside the area. Nothing to either of you if partner catches it. It starts you thinking tactically and do take a turn at throwing for your partner to hit, as this is all extra practice at reading the signals!

(ii) Rally with a partner, giving yourselves ten points every time you hit a backhand, but only one for forehands! You may certainly keep the rally alive by using the forehand, but as your target should be at least 100 points for beginners and 250 as you develop, you want to hit plenty of confident backhands!

(iii) Again rally with a partner but only one of you is hitting backhands. Aim is for this one player to do ten consecutive backhands, so the feeder gets practice in attacking the backhand wing and the other player hits plenty of backhand drives of all shapes and sizes!

(iv) Do the same practice as forehand practice (i) page 37 but this time hit across court to the backhand side.

(v) Co-operate with a partner in a rally of any number, but count only the backhands played by each of you; when four have been hit compete with your partner and try to win the point.

DOUBLE-HANDED BACKHANDS

Ask yourself these questions and answer honestly!

		Yes	No
(1)	Do you use a double-handed stroke at all?	Then read this section very carefully and decide your next moves by the way you answer!	Read this section anyway and know how to play effectively against the next two-hander you meet!

(Assuming you answered yes to question one, what are your next answers?)

(2)	Does your favourite player use a double-handed stroke?	Fine, then probably you would not want to change anyway!	Look carefully at the best double-handers you can find.
(3)	Did you start very young with a heavy racket? (or are you still very young with a heavy racket?)	Maybe, now that you are older and stronger you could let the other hand go a little (Think it out again in a year, or two).	You probably copied a good player known to you or just liked having two hands on the racket (for backhand usually).
(4)	Did you dislike trying to change grip from forehand?	A number of players put the second hand on the racket to strengthen up a weak grip still held in a forehand position.	Try your single-handed backhand. It could be good and anyway many double-handers often play a difficult to reach ball with one hand.

		YES	**NO**
(5)	Are you very quick about the court to make up for a shorter reach and, even more importantly, to get the precise position necessary for a good double-handed stroke?	Good, then you will be able to impose your double-hander on others.	You must quicken up as double-handed shots do not have a wide margin in which they may be played.
(6)	Do you feel that your double-handed shot merely answers shots played to you?	Then either position yourself better and use it effectively or change to single-handed shots!	What does it do then? If it does not even answer then you must improve it, or change to single-handed shots but if it does ask questions read section 7 below.
(7)	Do you try to work your game round to more and more shots on your double-handed side and to play them more and more aggressively?	Then you are probably a true double-hander in all respects.	Try your single handed shot over an extended period.
(8)	Are your hands close together?	Good.	You must bring them close together.
(9)	Do you bend and really get your weight into your shot?	Good.	You must do so, unless rather like Evert (and Borg a little) you spin on your feet as you play the shot.
(10)	Do you make certain you get the ball near thigh height?	Good.	High balls and low forward ones are difficult for double-handers.

3/7 Art-Gallery of the Double-Handed Art

Styles will always differ, but effort and technique will be remarkably uniform over many top players.

Note here how, although Tracy Austin's right-handed double-hander is a fully committed stroke like Jimmy Connors' left-handed double-hander, with body weight adding power via a good pivot, the equally world-class double-hander of Bjorn Borg seems to 'sling' the racket at the ball, with body slightly aloof, whilst the swift and elegant Chris Lloyd often appears to pirouette into shots, on occasions spinning on her right foot.

How Mrs Lloyd has taken her hands and racket well back behind and clear of her left hip, body turned side on to net

How Connors has bent low and kept the racket-face solid on impact, dominating the most rebellious ball.

All are 'correct', because relationship to **BALL** is good; the racket **(BAT)** is swung powerfully with control and the **BODY** assists carrying out the offensive, or defensive, decisions made by a champion's **BRAIN!**

Tour this Art Gallery and observe
how all four stars have the **BRAIN** registering the **BALL**, so closely watched, have the hands closely together on the **BAT (racket)** and obviously move the **BODY** urgently into position.

How Borg's straight arms and balance explicitly signify control and direction

How Miss Austin has really hammered even that difficult ball away to attack opponent

55

Summary

Remember it is always Ball first. The ball must go back over the net and into play. Bat second and Body third. Even if you should be in a terribly difficult off balance position with the body, the racket (bat) could still put matters right and play the ball properly if you use a little Brain.

Ball   Well away from it, take it fairly low, level in height with leading thigh.

Bat (Racket) Full take back, swing upwards at ball and lift over net with firm racket face.

Body   Bend well down on right foot, turn full sideways on to net, so that back of right shoulder is actually to the net and pivot round into hitting the ball like a swing-door.

Brain   Backhands are just as easy as forehands and often much more accurate and effective.

3/8 Early Preparation
Even when hurrying
forward to play a backhand
drive, be certain, like
Nastase here, that you get
your hand and racket back
early in preparation for a
strong forward swing.

4. GRIPS

Rarely do you find a chapter on grips! There are three main points overall on grip.

(1) Many top players have proved that virtually any grip may be used effectively.
(2) Every grip will have advantages and disadvantages.
(3) Grip is a very personal thing and many players stay in the particular grip with which they first played most strokes; some make a compromise as they learn from a coach, or by experience, that a change is necessary, others make a complete change and adopt a widely accepted grip for a certain stroke.

What must a grip do for you?
It must be
  – as natural as possible
             – as strong as possible
                         – as flexible as possible.
Look at the illustrations and the table overleaf.

Getting to grips with tennis rackets is often a slippery business! Some players use towelling-grips, which really need regular renewal; others roughen-up the edges of their grips; major tournaments often have sawdust, or resin available.

Perspiring palms are perfectly natural in reaction to tension on crucial points and during vital matches; be re-assured, therefore, that you are not 'sweatily' unique!

4/1 Grip Chart

Usual name	Racket-face kept at same photographic angle for change of hand position to be noted.	Features	Hand kept in same photographic position for the changes in racket-face angle to be noted.
Western Grip		Palm under racket handle.	
Eastern grip		Shake-hands. Palm behind handle.	
Continental (Chopper)		Hand slightly more on top of handle.	
Backhand		More or less 'continental' but more thumb support palm slightly more on top of handle even than 'continental'.	
Severe backhand		Thumb right along handle and palm severely turned over top.	
		**4/2** Note how little difference there is between the Chopper/Continental and the thumb strengthened backhand grip.	

Disadvantages	Advantages	Drives F/H	B/H	Service	Smash	Volleys F/H	B/H
Very difficult for low balls, especially volleying; huge change for backhand unless double hander used and no change. Frying pan approach to service.	Severe top-spin on forehand useful. Surprise reverse service and smash on occasions.	★	—	★	★	—	—
Racket would be a little too open on backhand; not quite snappy enough for most services.	Natural extension of arm. Every stroke may be performed with if it necessary. Strong, sensitive, especially for forehand drives.	★ ★ ★	★	★ ★	★ ★	★ ★ ★	★ ★
Too open a face for really good forehands, drives and volleys, unless wrist used.	Very flexible indeed on all strokes and strong on backhand. Hand held loosely and not too severely on top makes chopper grip for service.	★	★ ★ ★	★ ★ ★	★ ★ ★	★ ★	★ ★ ★
Less flexible than 'continental'	Stronger and good for beginners. Really good players especially left-handers could get extra severity of service with this grip.	—	★ ★ ★	★ ★	★	—	★ ★
Very restricted range of movements.	Strong.	—	—	—	—	—	—

Study the number of stars for confirmation of your own grips and/ or for considering any desirable modifications.

5. SERVICE

BRAIN

'Place the ball in the air, throw the racket at it!' If only you could get your brain to accept that simple definition of the service, the fear would go out of it straight away. These are the plus and minus features of service for your brain to consider.

Plus	Minus
(1) No-one but you really affects your service; your opponent has to wait and see what you hit him with!	(1) The wind and the sun (and even the score) might upset your calm control and rhythm!
(2) You have two chances, a first and a second service and you are always able to practise service alone and almost anywhere!	(2) No one ever really seems to practise their service as often as their other strokes, then there are complaints of it working poorly in a match!
(3) You decide where to stand and when and where to serve.	(3) You have to start behind the baseline and direct your shot into a small area of court.
(4) You can put the ball in the air in the best place to hit it.	(4) Unless you are very tall, you have to use a little spin for success.

You must have a positive approach, so what is your first objective? To clear the net by a reasonable margin and land the ball in the service court; on the first service hitting hard and taking a little risk going near the lines; on the second service to have a wider margin for error, but not give the opponent too easy a chance to pressurise you with a fierce return.

Look at illustration 5/1 and see the situation, then work out your answers under our usual headings. Concentrate on a simple top-spin service as a start, or very mild slice. Remember it is not possible to hit flat at first.

BALL

Place it where you want it. Hold it in fingers and thumb, firmly but nearer the tips of fingers rather than the palm. Hold one ball only if experimenting with throw-up. You should throw the ball about eighteen inches higher than hitting point, see illustrations for the various types of service. Height varies, too, as you get more adventurous; a glance at the service chart will key you in to the right height and our usual headings in the illustrations give you all the main points.

One rule of the game is particularly important and influences the way service is played. It is The Footfault Rule.

It indicates that during the service (from taking up position until the ball is struck) server may not –
   a) Change position by walking, or running

   b) Touch with either foot any area other than that behind the baseline and within the imaginary extensions of centre-line and side-line (See page 66).

The full Footfault Rule and all the other rules and how to score, etc., are available in The Rules of Tennis booklet from The LTA (See pages 110 and 111).

BAT (Racket)
The path and pace of the swing

Racket held in chopper grip and ball held against racket face.

Swing racket down and back as ball placed in the air and drop head of racket into a back-scratch position.

BODY
Footwork and balance

Stand in a throwing position slightly away from centre of baseline. Weight preferably mainly on rear foot.

Body weight starts to come forward over front foot as racket arm swings back and ball hand places ball carefully in air.

62

Racket does not touch back, but the angled face is ready to be thrown up at ball.

Grip and wrist have tightened to snap racket head up and over ball.

Racket has followed through to left side of body.

Right leg is about to pass left, elbow is up and body is reaching up for ball.

Eyes still on ball as body is stretched and its weight is helping spin and speed of service.

Balance is recovered on right foot and player should immediately be ready for any return.

5/2 The Service

BAT (RACKET)	Swing	PATH	Racket is taken down then	up into a close to the head throwing
		PACE	Smooth, very measured	start, dropping loosely
	Face	WRIST	Is very much used in service	almost opening palm up
		GRIP	Racket held like a chopper,	loosely allowing rackethead

**FOLLOW EACH
SUB-DIVIDED LINE
RIGHT ACROSS
BOTH PAGES**

BODY	Footwork	POSITION	You choose, so for singles be near centre, a little wider	in doubles, or if trying a severe angle
		STANCE	Slightly sideways on to	line – a throwing position
	Balance	WEIGHT	More on rear foot at start	then coming forward
		CONTROL	Steady, slow movement of both hands and body weight	until left hand puts ball in air

position, twirling behind head and shoulders,	then to stretch right up and slightly	over the ball before following through	fully forward and down left side.
into back-scratch position,	then the sudden snap of racket	to put speed and spin on ball	free-wheeling into follow-through
to sky as rackethead drops	then rotating slightly left to right	taking racket face across ball simultaneously snapping it	forward giving spin and speed.
to be dropped behind shoulders,	then tightening instantly to throw	racket head at and over ball, helping	strings 'grip' the ball for you.

feet comfortably apart, left toe slightly	pointed to line, right foot more parallel to it;	try to get on to left toe as ball struck,	right foot swinging freely through
as near as possible to line but	court must not be touched during service;	come well through with right foot	into court after ball struck.
on to front leg, knee bent preparatory	to straightening to help full high throw	of racket head as hips and shoulders complete	pivot and balance regained on right foot.
plus bent knee keeps balance and control	ready for swift movement of racket head	at ball during which there must be no falling	away to side or behind line

5/3 Angles for Better Service

In every game of every set of every match

the first, third & all ODD number points are commenced with **SERVER & RECEIVER** standing as here to the **"RIGHT"** of their respective courts

the second, fourth and all **EVEN** number points are commenced with **SERVER & RECEIVER** standing as here to the **"LEFT"** of their respective courts.

Server may stand anywhere behind baseline & within the dotted lines. Ball must be delivered diagonally across the court, landing in opposite service-box.

Receiver may stand anywhere on his own side of the net, but good positions for Right (R) and Left (L) courts are marked and depend a little on the regular length and speed of the service.

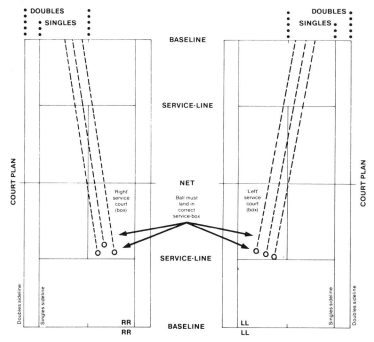

Server, positioned behind the baseline, has the net as a barrier 39 feet away and has to make the ball bounce before it reaches the service-line, which is a further 21 feet away, so, allowing a little for the diagonal across the court, a person about 6 feet tall, reaching well up to strike the ball with the centre of the racket-strings, would make contact as illustrated below.

Sectional diagram

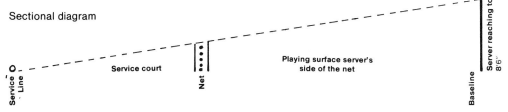

Obviously, even for such a tall person, the margin for error over the net is very small when a flattish downwards hit is employed. Also, the ball has to be projected off the racket extremely fast to overcome gravity's pull on it as it travels.

Therefore, right from the very start, try to make SPIN a vital ingredient of your service action, experimenting with, and adopting

a mild SLICE   and/or   **a mild TOP-SPIN**

Slice 'swings' ball over net with a 'late' fall, skidding a little on landing

Top-spin 'snaps' ball high up over net and it 'kicks' a little off ground

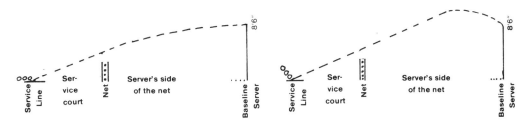

Service Line	Ser-vice court	Net

Server's side of the net — Baseline — Server — 8'6"

Even a modest amount of SLICE delays the drop of the ball, because the air displaced by the spin provides a 'cushion' underneath like a hovercraft. The easier of the spins for girls; left-handers use it 'wickedly'. Just 'drag' down the side of the ball.

Just a fairly gentle TOP-SPIN sends the ball up off the racket for better net clearance and the air displaced by the spin 'thrusts' down onto the ball, sending it quite attackingly into court. It is a simple 'brush' upwards on the ball, turning wrist outwards.

SLICE

Left hander   Right hander

12 o'clock

9 o'clock   3 o'clock

6 o'clock

Racket contact and movement on the ball
SERVER'S VIEW

TOP-SPIN

Left hander   Right hander

Racket contact and movement on the ball
SERVER'S VIEW

SLICE   TOP-SPIN

Certain services suit certain standards and situations. Look at the chart below which gives details of types of service and their features and especially note how many stars appear in the right hand columns. Three stars means it is very suitable: two fairly suitable; one only suitable on occasions and no stars means unsuitable.

5/4 SERVICE CHART (Three stars best)

Type of Service — Right-handed player (Left-handed reverse instructions accordingly.)	Direction & Height of ball placing		Clockface/racket-face movement	Spin and Security	Speed and penetration	SINGLES Experienced Player First Service	Second Service	SINGLES Inexperienced Player First Service	Second Service	DOUBLES Experienced Player First Service	Second Service	DOUBLES Inexperienced Player First Service	Second Service
Mild top spin	Relation to leading toes 9" to 12" in front and slightly to side	Relation to hitting point, about a foot higher	11 o'clock to about 1 o'clock	✱✱✱	✱		✱	✱✱	✱✱✱		✱	✱✱	✱✱✱
Mild Slice	Slightly more to side away from body still forward of toes	A little above hitting point	12 o'clock to 2 o'clock	✱✱✱	✱		✱	✱✱	✱✱✱		✱	✱✱	✱✱✱
Fast Slice	More forward again	Same	12 o'clock to 2 o'clock but snappier movement	✱✱	✱✱✱	✱✱	✱✱✱	✱✱✱		✱✱	✱✱✱	✱✱✱	✱
Kick (Heavy top spin on angled axis, giving breaking back effect)	Well back over head	Two feet above hitting point	Sharp brush from 8 o'clock to 12 o'clock	✱✱	✱✱	✱✱✱	✱✱✱	✱		✱✱✱	✱✱✱	✱✱✱	
'Flat'	Well forward of and slightly to right side of leading toes	A little higher than hitting point	Virtually straight into & on top of 12 o'clock but slipping to half past twelve!	✱	✱✱✱	✱✱✱		✱					

Service Chart Illustration

Placement of the ball for the main service deliveries for Right-handers.
(Left-handers, same positions in reverse.)
If you placed the ball in the air, but did not actually strike it, the landing points would be as below. Exact positions will depend upon age, height and strength, but this will guide your experiments and as you improve you should try, like top players, to place the ball more, or less, in the same spot for all service variations and, thus, confuse your opponents!

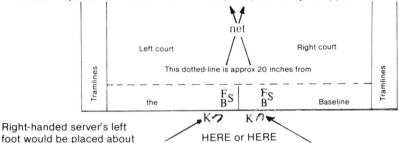

net

Left court   Right court

This dotted-line is approx 20 inches from

Tramlines   Tramlines

the $_B^F$S $_B^F$S Baseline

Right-handed server's left
foot would be placed about   HERE or HERE

B = Basic service, a very slight slice, or top-spin
F = Fast flattish service, ball about 18 inches ahead of toes
S = More pronounced slice, ball slightly to right side of body, but still well out from toes
K = More pronounced top-spin into 'Kick', ball dropping behind left heel.

'DO YOU PLACE IT?'

On the left, the side-on view of Server and, on the right, the back-view of Server, both give you further information and help in placing the ball in the air, effectively, for the main service possibilities.

The balls indicate the highest points of the various place-ups and where each would land, if allowed to fall. The arrows mark where contact with racket would best be made, unless you are an exceptionally good international player!

B for Basic service, slight top-spin, or slight slice, as preferred
F for Flattish, fast first service
S for a more pronounced Slice

K for a more pronounced top-spin into Kick

(Exact opposite for left-handers)

Study the various tips in all these illustrations carefully and then go on court and experiment, with as many balls, old or new, as you can find. Almost totally realistic service practice is possible entirely on your own! Just bear in mind that very new balls feel and act differently from very old ones and that, ideally, you are gradually trying to produce all types of service from very nearly the same place-up.

Follow up points on service and practices

BRAIN

Have a sensible outlook on service and use your strengths. If you are tall, look at illustration 5/5; see how well this player has got up on his toes, within a fraction of the line. Note that the server's body is leaning forward over the baseline into court following a ball placed well forward and the obviously strong racket-arm hurling itself at the ball and copy as in illustration 5/5 the flat hit downwards that can be achieved if you try hard

5/5 "Right up on your toes for fast 'flattish' serving"

5/6 Big first service!

Every ball, when hit, will spin slightly, but for this service try to bring your racket-face as 'flat' as possible right into the 'back' of the ball, a little above the 'Equator'. Your downward angle could be this severe if you are tall, reach well up and hit very hard to overcome gravity's pull.

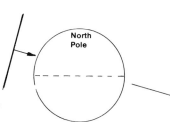

5/7 "So you think you have a flat service!"

Beware of hitting 'flat' the way some players think they do! **DO NOT** 'pull' your racket downwards with your arm, towards the 'South Pole', as this will impart a slowing-up backspin on the ball that you had intended as a flashing 'ace'!

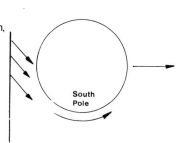

Note how server is contacting the ball well forward into court, some thirty inches nearer the net than the 'anchored' left foot.

70

and can stretch up to almost ten feet as this player does. If you are a shorter, or a tall person wanting to serve with a strong kicking action making the ball spin and turn off-line on bouncing, look at 5/8 and see how ball has been placed more over the head. The weight is back, the racket opened skywards and observe how in 5/8 it has brushed sharply and heavily up over the ball, which can be clearly seen going high off the racket, clearing net safely but being brought down into court by the top-spin. Also see page 67.

An alternative would be the slice, left-handers greatly favour this; the

5/8 Kick Service

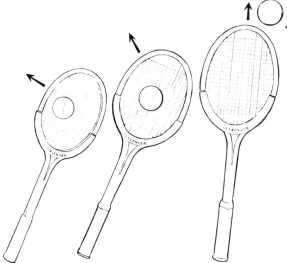

Look at the server in the photograph, and at racket angles and ball in the drawings, from the receiver's point of view.

Note how the racket-edge is angled for the face (strings) to brush upwards on the ball, ending with racket-face turned by wrist to be square on to the net, as ball **rises** off the strings. Ball is spinning towards receiver on an angled axis as shown here.

Ball movement off racket

ball is put out more to the front and side of the body and racket is sliced down and round ball as in 5/9. Whichever one you favour in any given situation, do not foot-fault as in 5/11)!

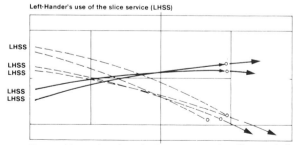

Left-Hander's use of the slice service (LHSS)

Vary position and angle and, of course, occasionally serve to forehand too!

5/9

Ann, serving here, is a **LEFT-HANDER** and this **SLICE** service action helps left-handers set up a very attacking situation against right-hander's backhands, swinging the ball wide out from either service-court.
RIGHT-HANDERS BEWARE!!

5/10 **RIGHT-HANDERS** should also make maximum use of the **SLICE** service.

Attack by swinging fast sliced services wide, or into an opponent's body.

Steady a second service with a little slice for control and to pose a small extra problem for the opponent.

The illustrations below are views of how Receiver would see a **RIGHT-HANDER'S SLICE SERVICE.**

THROW the racket at the ball, making the leading edge come round like a blade, whilst the strings cut down and round the ball.

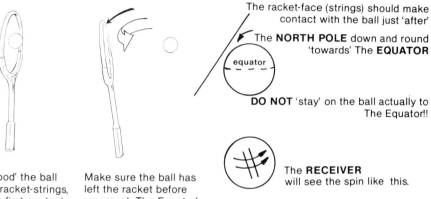

The racket-face (strings) should make contact with the ball just 'after'

The **NORTH POLE** down and round 'towards' The **EQUATOR**

equator

DO NOT 'stay' on the ball actually to The Equator!!

The **RECEIVER** will see the spin like this.

Try to 'hood' the ball with the racket-strings, i.e., make first contact just on top but do not cross 'Pole'.

Make sure the ball has left the racket before you reach The Equator!

5/11 However good your service action is, be certain not to spoil it with a **FOOT-FAULT!!** Server here is touching the line so the delivery is a fault.

73

Study the service chart, particularly noting uses of service and how a clock-face guide helps you understand spin applications. Imagine a clock just reachable and suspended as in illustration 5/12. You have to knock the clock off its pole and the same time move your racket face across the hours of the clock as in chart. Try it with just your hand!

5/12   Take your time for service, please!

Right-handers

'Flattish' **First** Service

Reasonably severe
'Kick' Service

Reasonably severe
'Slice' Service

Imagine that you are standing below a suspended clock and reaching up to smash it off its holder with your racket-face. For the various main services shown, the racket-strings should move **'CLOCKWISE'** across the face of the clock **STARTING** at the **MINUTE-HAND** and **ENDING** at the **HOUR-HAND!**

Left-handers

'Flattish' First Service

Reasonably severe
'Kick' Service

Reasonably severe
'Slice' Service

Imagine that you are standing below a suspended clock and reaching up to smash it off its holder with your racket-face. For the various main services shown, the racket-strings should move **'ANTI-CLOCKWISE'** across the face of the clock **STARTING AT THE MINUTE-HAND** and **ENDING** at the **HOUR-HAND!**

74

Finally, you must make use of the fact that on service you have two chances; live a little dangerously on the first ball in singles, worth a risk, or two; security but a little nastiness for opponent on second one! Think of this, a player who gets 100 per cent first services in is just not risking enough. For greater attack at his opponent – about 65 per cent would be the target – for second service you should aim for about 98 per cent – the occasional double-fault is a reasonable price to pay for a slightly more penetrative second service rather than an ultra safe dollydrop! For doubles you should try to get a very high percentage of first services in to court, as you have a partner in position waiting to pick up any loose returns.

BALL

Look at it when serving – many players forget this. Do not hit it, or attempt to, if you have placed it up badly. Bounce it, perhaps once, to settle yourself at the start of the service. Only put it in the air when you are balanced and ready.

BAT (RACKET)

Service is what is called a 'closed skill' – i.e., your technique is especially important because like golf, or bowls, or snooker, the situation does not change greatly as you are trying to play the shot, therefore, perfect your service technique even more than that of other shots. One vital item is grip. No one, no one at all, likes a 'chopper'-grip at first because everybody feels more comfortable with a frying-pan type of grip; that is because no one at first sees the service action for what (except for tall giants) it really is! The situation of court size and layout, the net and the footfault rule make it essential that you see the service action as
– a THROW of the racket head and a
    – BRUSHING of the strings on the ball.
There are three things to remember above all –
  (i) You must persevere with a chopper-grip – most other things in this book are advised – this is an order.

(ii) Keep aiming more and more to the right and hit higher and higher until one goes in with your horrible new grip.

(iii) Look at illustration 5/13 and see how essential it is to turn your wrist outwards.

BODY

Service needs strength and the body provides five major power generators from slow and heavy to fast and light in this order in the action.

Leg strength especially for lift and turn.

Hip and shoulder rotation on slice and fast services and tummy and back muscles especially on top-spin and severe kicking services.

Arm throw, like a fierce overarm throw upwards at a first storey window!

Wrist snap for really fast racket head work and control of strings across ball – and finally – fingers tightening as racket is brought into the ball.

The brain might understand various service techniques but the body will have to build up strength in these areas to perform them effectively, so remember that you can always practise service alone and only continual application will make the machine strong and smooth!

Service practices on your own

(1) Set up targets – large ones as in illustration 5/14 and try to hit them.

(2) Serve, if ball is in score yourself 15-love; serve again; ball again in, score is 30-love; serve again, ball into net, score is 30-15; serve again ball out, 30-all; serve again, ball in, 40-30; serve ball, in again, game to you and so on. Every time a good service, a point to you, a fault is a point to an imaginary opponent! If you are very weak, give yourself two services each point; if stronger, aim for a particular part of the court with a particular type of service in order to score a point.

(3) Divide the service-court in any way you like, perhaps three long channels as in illustration 5/14, and then aim like a golfer to see how many shots it takes you to do each 'hole' in turn.

5/13 Your Wrist is your Volume Control for Service

A

Hold the Chopper grip as in **A** on the left. Like that, the long bottom edge of the racket could hammer a nail into one of the lines on the court. Held high for throwing the racket into a first floor balcony, the palm of the hand would be towards your face.

Now look at **B**
See how the Chopper grip has been maintained, but the **WRIST** has turned the racket strings downwards. Held high for throwing at the "ball'-cony", your palm would be turned a little away from the face, *(C)*

B

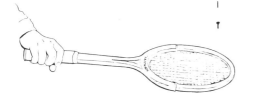

Use this **WRIST-TURN** as your 'volume-control' to obtain the desired balance between speed and spin.

Whilst using a flexible wrist to **THROW** your racket-head at the ball, be sure to keep your eyes actually watching the ball!

C

For sharper SPIN
Keep wrist more as in A
Start as in A & flick ·outwards and upwards to B

For swifter SPEED
Turn wrist more towards B
Do not flick wrist quite so severely from position A to B.

For FLATTISH FIRST SERVICE (fast), throw hard at and slightly downwards on back of ball, above 'Equator', flicking wrist from *(A)* position part way towards *(B)* position.

For right-handers it would be as illustrated and for left-handers exactly the same, but with the left hand.

Practices with an opponent

(4) Give yourself ten services. How many points can you win out of ten? If you serve six of them as faults, then you could at most only win four points; if you served ten terribly weak safe services your opponent could, perhaps, kill each one with his return and you might lose all ten, so try to balance between speed and safety. Your opponent then has ten services and tries to do better than you and so on, playing the point out normally each time when the server gets the service ball in to court.

(5) Service (normal first and second service, or just one service as appropriate to your standard and what you wish to practise) play out the point. If you win serve again; if you win again, serve again and so on until you lose a point when your opponent serves. Winner is the one who after, say, twenty minutes, has served the most times in unbroken succession.

(Both practices 4 and 5 done over full singles, or doubles court, as appropriate, or may be done down a long half of doubles court, using centre line as a side line, or done from one half-court across to the diagonally opposite half-court).

To close service for the moment note this, 'When in real doubt on service, serve your second ball first!'

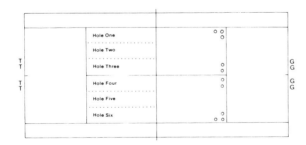

5/14 Service Practices

Player T is serving and aiming at the **TARGET CANS, HOOPS, BOXES,** etc. Player **G** is trying to play the "**GOLF COURSE**" as successfully as possible. Both may play at same time only if court is slow and their services are likewise!

6/1 Volleys are "punched"

6. VOLLEYS

BALL

So often less experienced players feel that their volleys let them down, or they avoid volleying because they have no confidence in the way they make the shot. Frequently, it is not the actual technique that is the problem at all, it is the basic positioning for the ball that is wrong, the attitude of mind, the preparation. There are really three distinctly different situations.

   (i) Already positioned in command at the net – very easy!

  (ii) Getting a commanding position at the net – from a position on court farther from the net – easy!

(iii) Getting caught en route – fairly easy!

6/2a Gaining a net position for Volleying

Singles

Look for opportunities, presented by short returns from your opponent, to get well inside the baseline to make your own drive, especially for Forehands, but, frequently, as **Here** on the Backhand, too.

Aim to place your drive low over net, fairly fast and deep, preferably to the opponent's weaker side, probably the Backhand.

Then follow the 'line' of your shot, as you approach the net, moving a little to the ball side of centre line.

'Gather' yourself for the **Volley** as you reach the net area. Go to 'meet' any return from your opponent, but do not rush blindly in and hope!

If you have to stretch wide to reach a well directed shot from your opponent, or if you have time on easier balls, bring the left foot over as indicated below, the foot hitting the ground at exactly the same moment as the racket strikes the ball. (On Backhand volleys the right foot would be the one coming across towards the ball.)

Sometimes the ball is straight at you, or near the body, so, make room for the shot by **Not** bringing the foot across. Also, very often on volley, the exchange of shots is so fast that there is little time for careful footwork. Remember, therefore, that, providing **Ball** is carefully watched, racket (**Bat**) is punched, or jabbed, firmly at ball and upper **Body** is as sideways as time and distance dictate, then your **Brain** can direct a good attacking, or defensive, volley to the best place, even with your feet square on to the net!

Make your approach drive all part of one smooth, swift, movement to the net!

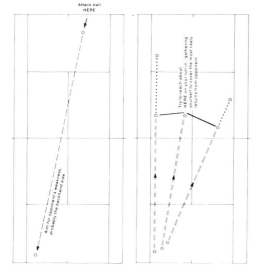

Punch the volley away for a winner

6/2b Gaining a net position for volleying

Doubles

In Doubles play, command of the net for volleying is even more vitally important. Server, (**S**) as below, usually delivers the service from a slightly wider position than in Singles. Server's partner, (**SP**) below, takes up a good volleying position immediately before the point commences, near net and covering tramline.

At the start of the point the receiving pair position themselves effectively, Receiver, (**R**) as below, maybe a little farther back on severe first services and perhaps edging towards net for weaker second service deliveries. To be ready for attack, or defence, Receiver's partner, (**RP**) as below, commences covering that half of the court, standing around the service-line. All positions vary slightly according to the players' standards, their strategy and the speed of court surface, weather conditions, etc.

Both Server and Receiver should try to play shots that allow them to move purposefully to join partner at the net. Server, Jennifer (**S**), has moved in after her service and has been caught by a good return, making her volley about halfway up the court. She will usually place this volley across court and move on in level with Nicky, (**SP**), who is closely watching the situation. Being an experienced player, Nicky is well in from tramline to threaten opponent's shot. Receiver will usually try to move in, too, and could well volley Jennifer's shot before it has a chance to land in the tramline as shown.

To examine them in turn –

(i) *Very easy in command at net.* Probably most often when you are server's partner in a doubles, or again in a doubles, you have, during play, managed to get to the net whilst your very good partner was doing all the work and you receive an easy ball! Try to react in order that the ball is struck

   – in front of the line of your body
   – but also slightly to the side of the body's position
   – well before the ball has started to dip down below net height (see illustration 6/4).

So, get in contact in front of you, slightly off centre and well above net height (do not lean over net to play it – illegal!).

(ii) *Easy* – get to the net to play it. The vital point here is that when you play the previous shot, perhaps a drive from just inside the baseline (see illustration 6/2a), you must make that shot a part of your move to the net; you must confidently decide to move to the net to volley, before you actually make that drive, then play the ball to a point that gives your volley a chance. You still have time to change your mind and stay back if your drive is not good enough but it is too late to decide to move forward to the net after you have seen where your drive has gone – a very important and often over-looked feature of volleying. What is really being said is that even a person with a poor volleying technique may get good results from volleying if they get into a good position confidently and early. What helps you gain this position?

   – make your approach shot (the stroke you are following to the net) strong and deep, possibly with some spin
   – in singles, if you have angled your shot to one side, follow the ball slightly to that side; in doubles if you have hit to an angle (illustration 8/13) your partner should cover the possible tram line return and you edge a little that way, nearer the net than your partner if at all possible.

A good point also to bear in mind on ball, especially in singles, is try and anticipate if your opponent will be able to make contact with the ball for his shot well inside any of the lines of his court. If so, he has a very good chance of passing you as you will not have long to pick up the direction of his shot as he is closer to you. However, if he is about on his own baseline, or just outside it, or well outside one of the sidelines, or even better well behind baseline and to the side of the court, then you should be able to pick off his shot easily and place a winning volley into the gap.

6/3 The 'Chances' of Successful Volleying
(In Singles especially, but relating also to Doubles)

Successful volleying so often depends less on the actual stroke technique and more on the overall situation. Look at the **AREAS** indicated below. Your **DRIVE** is played from somewhere in one of the **A, B, C** or **D** areas. You anticipate that your opponent will make contact with the ball somewhere in one of the **W, X, Y** or **Z** areas.

If you give each **AREA** certain **Values in points** and calculate these **Against** each other, it will give you a broad guide to your best option (i.e., take the points for **W, X, Y** or **Z** away from the points for **A, B, C** or **D** as below. **(0)** is your **Zero Option** (i.e., if points calculation results in a zero, or minus figure, going in to the net is either 'Very risky', 'Risky' or 'Slightly Risky', so you probably think only of getting back to **(0)**, your central, behind baseline position (singles), fast. However, if your 'score' in **ABCD/WXYZ** points is a plus quantity move-in, just as quickly, to the net position (N), following slightly to the side that the ball has travelled.

A = 2pts; B = 3pts; C = 4pts; D = 5pts.   W = 4pts; X = 4pts; Y = 3pts; Z = 0pts.

Your Volleying Tables

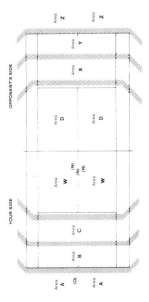

A(2) – W(4) = –2	Zero option; very risky to go to net	C(4) – W(4) = 0	It's risky, but you might really have to go in from C
A(2) – X(4) = –2	Zero option; very risky	C(4) – X(4) = 0	Slightly risky, but go in.
A(2) – Y(3) = –1	Zero option; risky to go to net	C(4) – Y(3) = +1	Go in; a good chance of a winning volley
A(2) – Z(0) = +2	Could risk going to net – very fast	C(4) – Z(0) = +4	Most definitely go in; excellent winning chance
B(3) – W(4) = –1	Zero option; risky to go to net	D(5) – W(4) = +1	You have to fight it out at the net with your opponent
B(3) – X(4) = –1	Zero option; risky to go to net	D(5) – X(4) = +1	Command net sensibly and you should win from here
B(3) – Y(3) = 0	Zero option, but risk net approach if match score/ conditions in your favour	D(5) – Y(3) = +2	Excellent chance of a winning volley
B(3) – Z(0) = +3	Take every opportunity to go to net	D(5) – Z(0) = +5	Excellent chance of a winning volley

Doubles situations would follow similar guidelines as to areas, but you would be more inclined to take an earlier risk to go to net, especially if your partner were already there. Remember that, in singles, or doubles, your 'approach to net' chances from ABCD are improved if your approach-drive has severe spin, speed, or angle, on landing in WXYZ. You take more chances of going in when the court surface is fast and/or slippy. Bear in mind, too, that you should take more of a risk when 40-Love up, than you do when 30-40 down!

Of course, figure out these equations before you go on court for your next vital match!

6/4 Volleys

BAT (Racket)
The path and pace of the swing

Reaching net area

See how the racket is prepared well forward of the body and ready to be lifted slightly above the anticipated hitting point.

Forehand volley (Fairly high)

It is clear that the racket is punching/jabbing into the ball, not flicking, or swinging, through; it is a short movement halted just after the hit.

BODY
Footwork and balance

Having reached the net area, the balance is gathered over the right foot pivot to move to cover the direction of the opponent's shot, this time a forehand volley.

The body turns slightly sideways for a close shot, more turn for a wide one; weight strongly forward onto front foot literally as ball hit.

Punch a winner

Study all three-forehand illustrations, noting how the high racket-head started in front, went back briefly, then firmly returned to where it started.

Backhand volley (Fairly low)

Exactly as in the forehand, the racket is punched firmly at the ball on the backhand; briefest of racket head movement, putting just a little backspin on ball.

Eyes glued to the ball. The 'crunch' down of the weight on to the front foot assists downwards 'punch' and volleyer springs back off front foot to cover next shot – if there is one it could be a backhand!

Weight again on to front foot as shot played, getting shoulder round; knees well bent to avoid scooping ball up and body perfectly steady, ready for quick recovery.

BAT

As with the drives and service the way you use the racket head is very important and is described, as before, under the heading of Bat above Illustration 6/4. The crucial difference on volley is that you should not swing, or throw, or flick, the racket at the ball but play it with a short action. Get any word into your head that encourages that, such as *jab, punch, block, or even, hammer.*

The movement is stopped short – there is little backswing and virtually no follow-through.

(iii) *Fairly Easy.* Very often you get caught by an opponent's return as you are en route to the net; the ball may be quite low, too. Here try to stop your run and crouch and crunch into a good volley position, leaving room for your racket to control the low ball and keep it low over the net with a little backspin (similar to a golfer getting to the hole from a bunker!). Illustration 6/4 (backhand volley).

BODY

Grip firmly on impact but use wrist, just a fraction, dragging ball

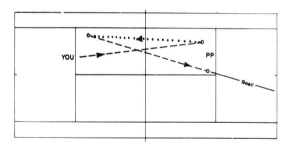

6/5 Volley Goals

You and your practice-partner **(PP)** both start near service-line, using just the one half of the width of the court. Take it in turns to commence a 'point' and move nearer the net as rally progresses. Each shot must land in the respective service courts. Your shots are the broken lines, the opponent's **(PP)** shots are the dotted lines. You score a goal by volleying into service court and making ball go on past an opponent by sheer speed, angle, or positioning.

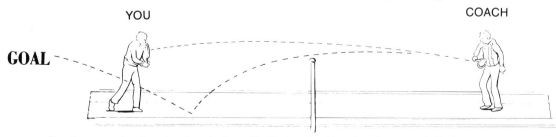

Practice may, of course, be done just as effectively using the other longways half of the court as illustrated but make certain that you have some longer rallies and that you beat the coach!

downwards imparting a little backspin simultaneously with weight sinking forward on the front foot.

Volley practices (see illustrations 6/5 and 6/6)

(1) Imagine the service court as your goals. Volley sharply with your practice-opponent trying to score a goal by volleying past him but within the extended lines of the service court.

(2) Start outside the service court and play a moderate ball to land in the diagonal service court, your practice-opponent being just outside it. Both move to the net volleying crisply into the diagonal service courts. Score as in tennis or table tennis.

BRAIN

Like a drive and a service, be aware of what is possible for you; getting the ball in court and making things difficult for your opponent are the priorities. However, on volley there should be many opportunities to finish the point firmly, not wildly, remembering that you are not looking "to rally continually on the volley," you are thinking of hitting an outright winner. At an early level of play, most of your volleying will be done in doubles and here the two golden rules are

  (i) Aim to play the ball to the side of the court where the opponent is further from the net.

 (ii) If in doubt,
     don't hit it out,
     solve the riddle,
     hit down the middle!

6/6 **Good doubles volley practice**

You and practice-partner **(PP)** again use just the service-courts, this time diagonally. 'Goals' could be scored again but often play points; 21-up, serving (underarm) five points each in Table Tennis fashion, or serving alternative games with Tennis scoring. Practise across opposite diagonal as well, or two other players may safely and effectively play a separate game across the other two service courts.
Your shots are shown as broken lines and your practice-partner's shots are dotted.

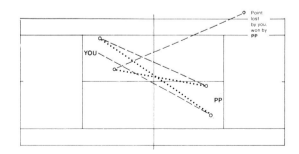

7. ANALYSIS AND CORRECTION OF ERRORS

Analysing your own errors and correcting them. Firstly, remember that a one-off error does not really matter – anyone champion, or beginner, will have an off day, will have a momentary lapse of concentration, will put an easy ball out, or in the net. Over and over again a good shot from your opponent will force an error from you, so, do not feel that each and every mistake must immediately be pounced upon and scrutinised with worry and concern! Remember, too, that the simplest way of all to correct an error is to do the complete opposite next time! For example, you have hit three balls in succession just into the net when merely trying to get a reasonable length – right, try next time to hit the ball half-way up the stop netting behind your opponent! Or, you have put four balls one after the other over the baseline, so, aim the very next attempt to hit the top of the net! Often these simple opposites will work wonders, but to be just a little more scientific look at the Analysis and Correction of Errors Chart.

Tennis at the top is no game for weaklings! That ball must go back! The determination and effort, so obvious on Ken Rosewall's face, is a good indication of why he was the World's number one professional player for so long and why he still reached The Wimbledon Men's Singles Final at the age of forty!

Note

The columns on the next two pages will help you discover many common faults, although all will not be included. Get a more experienced friend to look at your three main strokes, forehand and backhand drives and your service. Get someone to film, or video-record you. Best of all arrange to attend sessions with a coach, preferably a full professional, usually a registered member of The Professional Tennis Coaches' Association of Great Britain (PTCA), or if not in Britain a member of the country's own professional coaches' association.

Analysing Your Errors On The Major Strokes
Possible Causes Under Regular Headings

Fore hand Drive Error	BALL	BAT SWING Path	Pace	FACE Wrist	Grip	BODY FOOTWORK Prep-aration	Stance	BALANCE Weight	Control	BRAIN (possible corrections)
Ball in net. Ball lacks power, lands too short	Taken too low	Not a long enough take back. Not enough lift	Too late in take back or too slow in build up	Too turned over to ground	Too 'Western'	Too far back from ball	Leading foot not placed or placed far too far across	Fallen forward too soon	Knees bent have not steadied stroke	Bend lower, get lower long edge of racket under ball, hit a little harder and will it over baseline!
Ball over baseline. Ball floats or blasts into netting, goes too high and weakly	Taken too low, & scooped up, taken too high & not closed or sliced down	Too much lift, or slice; too 'floaty'	Too much power, perhaps hurriedly applied	Too open to sky, causing strings to chop ball skywards	Too open a grip, 'Continental' or too loosely held	Too close up to ball	Too open a stance	Fallen backwards ball taken behind body	Knees straightened too sharply and balance lost	Hit a little less powerfully aim for top of net, get more top-spin on ball
Ball to left of intended target area	In attempting too much top spin racket pulls ball across	Too much across body	Too early reaching ideal hitting point	Flicking loosely through	Maybe an over-correction of an 'open' grip	Too far away from ball	Too 'open'	Weight fallen to left side	Knees not bent to balance body	Aim to right of target, prepare less hurriedly
Ball to right of target	Ball behind body when hit	Racket scoops across back of ball spilling it out to right	Too late in build up	Wrist cocked back, not allowing racket head to be straight with arm movement	An open grip causing a scoop	Body brought too near ball	Leading foot too far across and no room for racket swing	Weight fallen onto back foot	Body has gone too straight into ball's bounce path instead of on a line to behind and to side of bounce	Get into a position more to side of ball's path; hit ball on line with, or in front of, leading thigh; aim to left of target

Backhand Drive into net and over baseline situations are similar to Forehand, but reverse left and right situations, i.e., ball to right of target becomes ball to left, then read off possible errors as for Forehand). (Weak, floaty type backhands dropping short are often caused by too open a grip – not enough change made from a western (frying-pan) forehand grip, so racket face skims under ball and player has to drag ball from behind him instead of strongly hitting out in front.

Service Error

Service Error									
Ball in net	Placed too far forward	Not a long enough build up	Not enough speed in racket head throw at ball	Angled too much downwards	Frying pan	Too hurried	Too square on to net	Forward too soon	Weight has leaped and caused racket to crash down on ball	Ball placed higher and farther back; build up a fuller racket head throw and brush ball upwards
Ball over service line	Placed too far back behind head and possibly contacted too low	Racket cramped when hitting ball and still travelling far upwards	Too fast, too soon	Racket has not struck enough of the top of the ball	Possibly frying pan racket face sliding down back of ball making it rise like a hovercraft	Too hurried	Probably also too square on to the net	Weight too far back	Weight has sunk down too soon dragging racket below ball	Aim higher. Aim for top of net. Place ball further forward and bring racket head through quicker and more on to the top half of ball.
Ball swings out to server's left (right-hander)	Placed too far forward; too far to left, or sometimes too far to right & player over compensates	Racket comes 'round-arm' into side of ball not thrown at ball from behind head	Build up too fast; too sliced	Has not turned outwards to present flatter racket-face to back of ball	A recent change to chopper could cause this	Too intent on setting up a heavily sliced service. Standing too far out to side when serving to right court, or standing too near centre when serving to left court	Too square	Too far forward. Off balance when ball struck	Body has pivoted too soon & racket has hit right side of ball with too much slice	Try to hit more of the side of the ball nearer to you and turn wrist outwards. Aim well to right
Ball goes too far to the right of server (right-hander)	Placed too far back; too far to left	Racket head comes too far over left side of head & is cramped in hitting ball	Possibly fast racket head trying to put too much top spin on ball	Too opened out & travelling upwards on ball too much	Too flat and racket hitting inside (nearer body) and underside of ball	Too square; perhaps standing too near centre line in right court, or too near sideline in left court. Trying too hard for a winner	Too sideways on to baseline	Falls backwards as service played	Body & racket face too much on left side of ball	Place ball further forward. Aim more to the left. Snap racket more around outside of ball. Get weight high and 'over' ball

8. BALL, BAT, BODY AND BRAIN FOR THE LAST TIME!

BALL

There are, of course, many other effective ways in which you can get the ball into your opponent's court in addition to the major strokes, forehand and backhand drives, service and volleys, already described.

Lob

One of the best ways of –

    (i) Clearing the danger when the opponent is breathing fire and disaster at you from close to the net – keep lobbing him back off it and he will puff more like an old man and less like a dragon!

    (ii) Giving yourself more time to recover your position.

    (iii) Returning service occasionally in a doubles over server's partner's head.

Play the stroke as if driving, but open out the racket face and follow-through upwards. If the ball is very fast, drag the speed off it by slicing the ball upwards.

Aim as high as you like in defence and just over opponent's head (with a little top-spin if possible) in attacking situations, always trying to bounce the ball near the baseline and slightly to the non-racket side of your opponent. (Illustration 8/1).

In SINGLES aim your lobs for here	In DOUBLES aim your lobs for here

Singles

RHS

RHS

RHS

RHS

Doubles

Doubles

8/1 Place your Lobs

If you are lobbing a right-handed opponent, the most awkward areas for you to attempt to land your lobs are over a right-handed-smasher's (**RHS**) left shoulder as below. The exact opposite is the case when playing left-handers.

Smash

Like a service action except that:

  (i) You have not put the ball up so you have to move very quickly to get into position under the ball, with at least the upper part of the body sideways on to the net.

 (ii) The ball is accelerating and, therefore, must be watched even more closely than other shots when it is decelerating

(iii) You are near the net and you have the whole court to hit into, so place your smash, do not just frantically hit it!

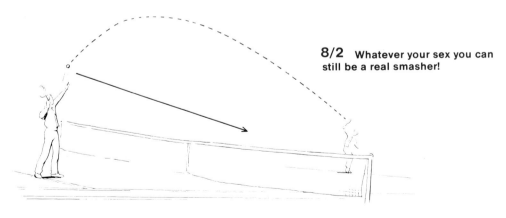

8/2 Whatever your sex you can still be a real smasher!

93

A few tips for better smashing:

– believe in it!

– be in a place near the net that would allow the ball to drop on your non-racket shoulder if you did not smash it first.

– for a long deeper lob that you have to take well back in the court, let it be dropping over your racket shoulder.

– reach up and pluck the ball out of the air, turning your wrist to flatten the racket face in the direction in which you intend your smash to travel.

– try not to bring your racket across the line of the lob but position your body so that the arm drags it down with the minimum chance of error.

– sight the ball by raising your free hand high and homing in on it. (Illustration 8/2).

– leave all the acrobatic jumping to the acrobats!

Drop-shot (More a singles than a doubles shot)

A telling way to finish a long rally. At first only risk drop-shots when you are fairly near the net and when your opponent is well back from the net. Try to deceive your opponent into thinking you are going to drive normally then gently slow the racket action, chop slightly down the back of the ball, delicately floating it quite high over, but trying almost to split the ball by actually dropping it on the net itself. Too often players send off a drop-shot on a low flight over the net – the trajectory should be steeply up and then the drop of the ball is almost as if falling down the cliff face of the farther side of the net! Any drop-shot that does not have its second, third, fourth, and, even, fifth bounce inside the service court is a failure!

8/3 Devastating drop-shots do wonders for your confidence and also develop a more sensitive 'feel' on all shots

8/4 Dink Shots
'Drop' the racket and weight down into ball, as here, 'sliding' the ball low over the net, but with fair pace, in order to make a net-rushing opponent volley weakly upwards, or to make the ball slip past him like a thief in the night! Hit softly but think loud!

Other strokes

There are other shots too to be experimented with, lob-volley, stop (or drop)-volley, half-volley (really only in emergencies) and dink shots.

Dink shots are worthy of a special mention. The aim is to slide the ball down low over the net so that it would go near an intending volleyer's feet. (Illustration 8/4). Very useful counter to a net attack and extremely effective as a doubles service return.

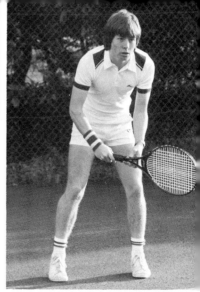

8/5 Return of Service

You may stand where you like to return service, but usually just behind the baseline, near the tramlines, in both right and left courts, as above, proves to be the most effective position in singles and doubles. Move in a little if your opponent's service is weak.

Try to make a fullish driving, attacking, return, moving quickly to use your strongest wing, forehand, or backhand, but, sometimes, your opponent's service is so severe that you will prepare only a short swing, endeavouring to 'block' the ball back as shown on the left. Steady consistent returns boost you and demoralise an opponent!

Receiving first service in right court, stand at **RS1**. For second service **RS2** and for beginners with weak backhands, take **WBH** positions.

Receiving first service in left court, stand at **RS1**. For second service **RS2** and for beginners with weak backhands, take **WBH** positions.

Return of service

To end with one of the most important shots in the game – return of service. This is never given the attention it deserves. Look at illustrations 8/5 and 8/13 and see where best to stand. Crouch eagerly but calmly, ready to move body and racket in any direction and particularly with knees bent. The nearest shot to a return of service is a drive, but it is different.

Why?   (i) You are rarely running very far first.

        (ii) The ball has pitched down at you, often with considerable top spin, or slice.

      (iii) In doubles especially, you often have to avoid opponents attacking at the net.

      (iv) You do not have much time to build up a swing.

So –   (i) Shorten the full drive movement a little, almost blocking a really fast service back into court.

      (ii) Grip very firmly to control the racket face.

      (iii) Try hard to place the return effectively, swinging fully through when this is possible.

      (iv) Vary the type of return endlessly and imaginatively.

      (v) Get the weight going forward into the shot somehow even when very rushed, by bending knees and sinking forward into the shot.

The steady, relentless, accurate, returner of service is an opponent to be feared!

Practice with the ball

How you use a tennis ball (or better still dozens of tennis balls!) in practice is very, very important to your development. In each early chapter there were suggested practices suited to each stroke. Now on these next few pages in words and court-plans (8/6–8/11) are some higher more sophisticated practices. The correct term for most of them is functional practices, because they enable you to put yourself into a true game situation and they perform this function over and over again, but the name does not matter, just make certain there is a will to do well!

Pressure practices

An essential element of practice is pressure; a pressure on you higher than you will normally experience in the game. If you are striving to perfect a technical point (a grip change, a new swing pathway, or a different body position to the ball) do not overdo the pressure; you will destroy the skill level attained, but put more and more pressure on as the stroke gains confidence – trust your technique and really scurry! What does pressure training achieve?

  (i) It improves strength, speed and stamina, exactly in keeping with the game's demands.

 (ii) It helps the player to detect what shot is coming and answer it quicker and more effectively.

(iii) It makes for quicker recovery to a good position.

(iv) It helps a player maintain a particular standard of performance longer before fatigue lowers it.

The simplest form of pressure training would be for a coach, or partner, feeding in a rally (or even throwing) so that balls go to player shorter, longer, wider, finer, higher, lower, faster, slower, spinning, or at shorter intervals. The player receiving the shots is also under slightly more pressure if the coach, or feeder, moves up from feeding on the baseline and volleys crisply from the net.

However, two real pressure training exercises would be as follows:

  (i) One player is in the driving position, behind centre of baseline roughly intending to cover the whole of the singles court. Two players are on the opposite side of the net volleying to this singles player, doing their best to make each ball difficult, but just playable in relation to the previous shot. The volleyers try to keep the rally going at all costs, the single player tries to make a 'safe' winner, i.e. the value of the practice is lost if the feeders kill the ball too often and if the player under pressure just hits desperately and wildly.

 (ii) Exactly as for (i) but with the single player at the net and the feeders on the baseline. Subtle lobs and dink shots and great variation of pace make this practice even more effective. In both practices another ball is put into play as soon as one ball goes dead and an attempt is made to replenish the ball supply as quickly as possible. Intensity is the watchword and about ten minutes really intense work for each single player involved is better than longer in more 'ragged' fashion.

If you were lucky enough for five players all to agree to practise together, then the feeding pair can be replaced by the other pair with a fresh supply of balls to keep up continuity.

Attitude

Whilst you are doing pressure training think of something Hannibal once said,

'When you are winning give your opponent no rest; when you are losing give yourself no rest!'.

8/6   Functional Practices – Pressure Training

Skill is Technique + Timing + Tactics, therefore, do not just practise the parts, practise the whole! Keep your practice 'functional', either by intensifying the whole game situation as in Pressure Training, below, or by spotlighting a whole situation within the game and repeating actions and reactions within such situations over and over again, as highlighted for you in Figures *8/7-8/11*

In Pressure Training, two, or more, players are putting one player under appropriately severe pressure, according to standard.

Look at the illustration below. **PP** is the pressured player and **F/1** and **F/2** are the feeders, all in their starting positions. The dots are the feeders' shots and the continuous lines are PP's returns. **F/1** commences with the first drive (1**(D)**), **PP** volleys (**(V)2**), **F/1** drives again (3**(D)**), PP volleys sharply across court. (**(V)4**, in answer to which **F/2** plays a deep lob and so on. Feeders try to vary the shots, making everything just possible for **PP** to play. PP's objective is to make a sure singles court winner off every shot if possible, but with two good feeders covering that court it is tough stamina and strength training, as well as developing tactical responses.

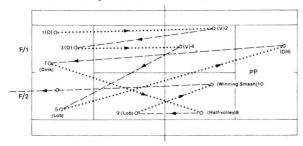

This pressure training practice, especially in the case of higher standard players, could also be done effectively with the feeders at the net volleying and the pressured player on the baseline. A group of, ideally five, players could make the exercise even more intensive by two pairs of players taking it in disciplined turns to keep a continuous stream of shots directed at the one pressured player. A good ball supply is needed by the feeders who must try just as hard as **PP**. Obviously all take turns at being **PP**, the pressured player!

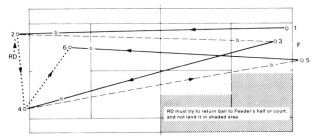

RD must try to return ball to Feeder's half of court, and not land it in shaded area.

8/7 Running drives and ranging control

Feeder **(F)** attempts to give strong but playable drives ranging alternatively wide across to forehand and down to backhand continuously for the Running Driver **(RD)** to return severely but always back to Feeder's longways half of the court. Change roles after about 5 min. and also take a turn using other half of court.

8/8 Backhand drive and intercepting volleys

When four players are together do not always just play a doubles. Try this practice and really hit those backhands.

BX and **BZ** are attempting to hit a powerful consecutive rally of six backhands across court avoiding the volleyers (**VW** and **VY**). To avoid giving an easy volley, the backhands have to be lifted drives skimming across the net. Volleyers must try to intercept and make winners, but if they go too soon, may be passed down the tramlines as player has been here, half anticipating the dotted line return.

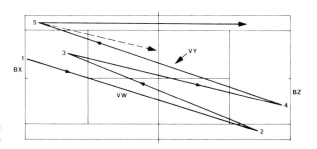

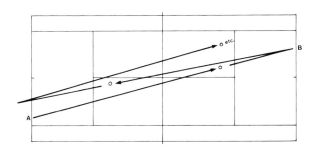

8/9 Low top-spin driving

Two players (**A** and **B**) hit firmly cross-court trying to make ball land just inside the diagonally opposite service-court, or thereabouts, with ball struck hard enough to carry on to baseline. This is a co-operative rather than competitive practice, but really drive the ball **hard** and **low** and these aims will inevitably lead to top-spin. Practise across backhand diagonal, too.

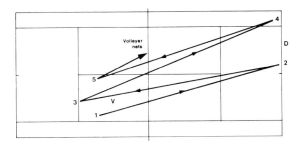

8/10 Volley to drive

Follow up the friendly co-operation of Practice *8/9* with the fierce competition of Volley to Drive. One player (**V** for Volleyer) comes nearer to net and tries to play good deep volleys diagonally at Driver (**D**), who hits low and fiercely (occasionally subtly, too!) for the volleyer's feet inside the service-court.

Score points (21-up, or Tennis scoring) and take turns driving and volleying and use other diagonal, too. Volleyer could even start point off with a service. Four players could do it as two doubles pairs. One pair in the service courts volleying diagonally, or straight, and the other pair driving.

8/11 Service squares

Play a full game but just using the four service-courts. This greatly helps your, touch, your appreciation of angles, quick recovery, subtle backspin, sharp top-spin and played properly is like exhausting chess! Serve underarm across court, alternating sides and service as in a normal game, etc. Arrowed lines show pathways of the various shots. The starting positions for both players are indicated as **Y** for you and **PP** for your practice partner.

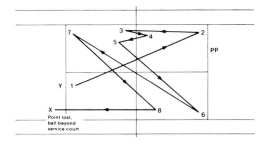

101

The Ball, Bat, Body, Brain, they are all involved in spin.

Spin is merely the movement of a ball about an axis in flight.

It has not so far proved possible for a human being to hit a tennis ball without spin.

Certain tactical situations demand an attempt to impart the maximum amount of any desired spin.

Certain tactical situations demand that the ball be hit with the minimum of spin.

A ball can only spin one way at any one time and, except in freak winds, on any one journey.

A ball can only spin either 'forwards', or 'backwards', relative to flight, around an axis

The spins below are all seen by you coming towards you and are the only four 'pure' spins, being on vertical, or horizontal, axes.

Topspin

Ball will sharply rise then dip into ground with high bounce

Lefthand 'side'

Ball will approach curling right of receiver, continuing its curl on bouncing

Righthand 'side'

Ball will approach curling left of receiver, continuing its curl on bouncing

Backspin

Ball will hang in flight and skid, or sit up, on bounce

However, a ball usually spins on an angled axis, 'forwards' round the axis giving 'impure' topspin (or, severely in service, 'kick'), or 'backwards' round the axis giving 'slice', sometimes 'chop', both being 'impure' backspin.

Kick (As in a right-hander's service)

Has topspin characteristics and on drives is nearly pure topspin

Topspin is imparted by racket coming up on ball. Ball starts on upper strings and leaves racket from lower strings.

Slice (As in a right-hander's backhand drive)

Has backspin characteristics, occasionally as if mixed with 'side'.

Backspin is imparted by racket coming down on ball. Ball starts on lower strings and leaves racket from upper strings.

Both wind and surface can increase and decrease the effects of spin.

Topspin is essentially aggressive and penetrative.

Backspin can be used aggressively, but is on balance more defensive.

BAT (RACKET SELECTION)

Nearly all tennis players operate at some time in their careers with an unsuitable racket. There are three ways to avoid this.

(1) Look at the chart and note how certain sizes of rackets link with ages, etc.
(2) Ask your coach.
(3) Ask at a sports shop with a knowledgeable tennis assistant. (Take this chart with you!).

DO NOT –

(1) Play with uncle's, or father's, or mother's, old racket at the age of ten, or eleven, unless you have used it for years and strengthened with it, or unless it is your only chance of having a racket to play with at all!
(2) Ask just anyone who happens to play tennis seriously and well – many really good players do not know what is available and suitable for younger, weaker, enthusiasts.

Do play Short-tennis if you are young, as a lead into larger equipment.

Steel rackets will move through the air quickly and aid service and volley especially; wooden rackets give a more traditional feel of the ball and probably save you from tennis elbow more readily by absorbing the shock of impact better, although in theory this is not so! Large headed rackets allow more margin for error.

Other equipment

If you look and feel clean and smart on court you will play better and with no lack of confidence. Break-in new shoes and socks before serious match play; woollen socks absorb perspiration better; warm-up in a track-suit; protect gut stringing with a headcover; keep an infrequently used racket in a press.

Racket Selection Chart

Normal, Midi and Maxi Size Heads

Three frame qualities in most makes:
Natural gut stringing.
All Weather.
Man-made (cheaper fibres).

JUNIOR

Junior Racket Range:
26 ins and less

ADULT

Adult Racket Range:
All 27 ins long

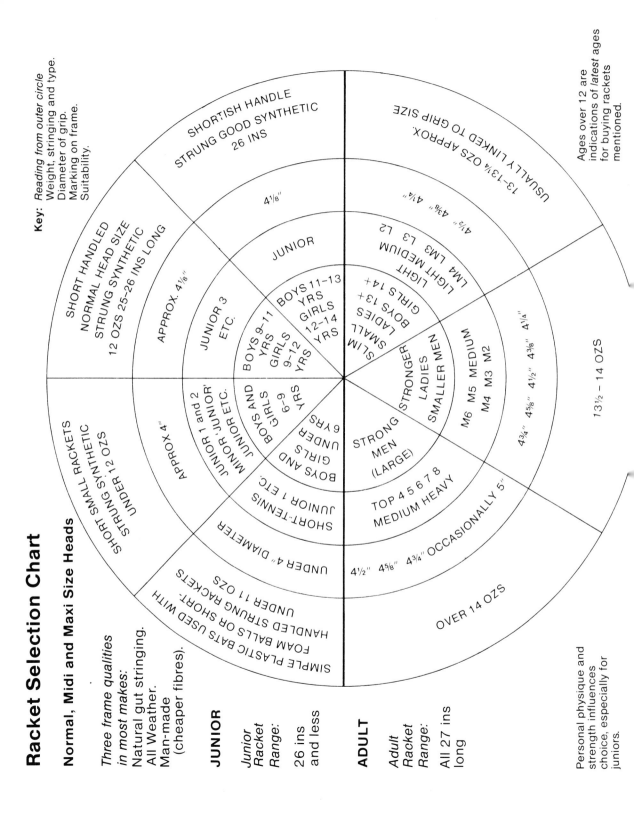

Key: *Reading from outer circle*
Weight, stringing and type.
Diameter of grip.
Marking on frame.
Suitability.

Ages over 12 are indications of *latest* ages for buying rackets mentioned.

Personal physique and strength influences choice, especially for juniors.

SHORTISH HANDLE STRUNG GOOD SYNTHETIC 26 INS

SHORT HANDLED NORMAL HEAD SIZE STRUNG SYNTHETIC 12 OZS 25–26 INS LONG

SHORT SMALL RACKETS STRUNG SYNTHETIC UNDER 12 OZS

SIMPLE PLASTIC BATS USED WITH FOAM BALLS OR SHORT-HANDLED STRUNG RACKETS UNDER 11 OZS

USUALLY LINKED TO GRIP SIZE

13–13¼ OZS APPROX.

13½ – 14 OZS

OVER 14 OZS

4⅛"

APPROX. 4⅛"

APPROX 4"

UNDER 4" DIAMETER

4½" 4⅜" 4¼"

4¾" 4⅝" 4½" 4⅜" 4¼"

4½" 4⅝" 4¾" OCCASIONALLY 5"

JUNIOR

JUNIOR 3 ETC.

JUNIOR 1 and 2 MINOR 'JUNIOR' ETC.

SHORT-TENNIS JUNIOR 1 ETC.

LIGHT MEDIUM LM4 LM3 L2

MEDIUM M6 M5 M4 M3 M2

TOP 4 5 6 7 8 MEDIUM HEAVY

BOYS 11–13 YRS GIRLS 12–14 YRS

BOYS 9–11 YRS GIRLS 9–12 YRS

BOYS AND GIRLS 6–9 YRS

BOYS AND GIRLS UNDER 6 YRS

LIGHT BOYS 13+ GIRLS 14+

SLIM SMALL LADIES STRONGER LADIES SMALLER MEN

STRONG MEN (LARGE)

BODY

To play good tennis you have to be fit; you do not play good tennis in order to be fit. Think of the seven 'S's. Your body's requirements are

Speed   **Strength**   **Stamina**   **Suppleness**

acquire these

Sensibly   **Steadily**   **Six-fold.**

Six sections of daily exercises, gradually increasing repetitions from only one, or two, at start. Vary your schedule, choosing exercises from each section.

(1) Warm-up; jog gently; loosen shoulders; skip.

(2) Stand square; twist upper trunk; bend from side to side.

(3) Do some press-ups on finger-tips, pull-ups or sit-ups.

(4) Lie on tummy and lift head well back, or gradually try to flick head and legs back like a salmon.

(5) Do a 'potato race' with six tennis balls at farthest corners and sides of a normal lawn, or on half a tennis court, or do short shuttle runs from tramline to tramline for a minute, then increasing.

(6) Run around the court 30 times, then next day 31, and so on, always keeping inside 12 minutes; once a week go for a three, or four, mile cross-country run.

After six weeks you should be basically fit. Now increase the repititions and add very intensive pressure practice on court and intensive matchplay. If you feel real distress at any time, check with your doctor. Push yourself, but sensibly and steadily build up; rest completely at the peak of a cold, or flu, etc.

BRAIN

There are two major items that should be covered under this final look at your *tennis-brain.*

  (i) The tactics you use.

 (ii) The way you link into the world of tennis in the county in which you live.

Tactics

The true and original definition of tactics is a military one, and is *the movement of forces on the field* and tennis is very much a pleasant and exciting battlefield for you to test your strength of character, courage, stamina and generalship, against a usually, friendly enemy! A very famous general (Clausewitz) said in his book (on war) that you should always try to bring your maximum force to bear on your enemy's weakness. Very good for tennis, too! How might we do this?

Possible tactical headings for singles

Imagine you are going along the shelves of a supermarket that is selling you possible ways of returning the ball, increasing in price. The tennis situation is the price you can afford! If your opponent has put you in a really poor position you have to take the cheapest offer and so on. On the shelf you see, 'get the ball back into the court whatever happens' – buy it! However, if you would have some change to spare, look farther along and see 'restrict your opponent's next choice of shot' – slightly better is it not? Still money over? i.e., the tennis situation you are in is not a desperate one, so buy offer number three, marked 'put real pressure on your opponent' – or even go right to the most expensive – and make an outright winner! Understand, you choose the reply to your opponent's shot that is the most telling and expensive that you may make in the circumstances. If the ball always goes back into court you cannot lose, which is a good start; now make more positive moves to win the point. Move into a good position yourself as soon as you can and always recover back into a good position, or the best you can possibly manage.

Move your opponent around the court to have to play the ball in awkward spots, hit to a good length and try to bring your strength (your best shots) to bear on his weaknesses (aimed at his poor shots, perhaps the backhand?). Deceive and surprise your opponent; when he rushes to cover a gap, hit it just exactly where he has moved from; sometimes serve a very slow first service; hit hard at him (not to hurt him, it will be a very poor player indeed who actually lets the ball hit them!) when he is at the net to force an error off his racket, instead of always going for the passing shot.

Remember, it is how and where you actually make your opponent hit the ball that is important, not always where you make it bounce; ask yourself in which situations do you want to put over a slow, high ball bouncing near the baseline and where do you want a faster ball bouncing perhaps a little shorter, but rushing on, penetrating well over your opponent's baseline?

Watch, listen, read and absorb the tactics of better players, concentrate hard and you will become a good general, too, but be yourself; if you want to play more carefully than others, then do so, but attack when you should; if you like a little risk and speed in your play have it, but remember the hardest hitting top players put the ball into court!

Doubles

You cannot be so personal in doubles. You are a pair now and you must team-up in all respects with your partner. So, get into good basic positions (illustration 8/13) and as the court is only a little wider than in singles, try to get to the net and cover it with your partner. The opponents might lob you but if not, there are only really two dangerous gaps to cover in every situation, so cover these two as in illustration 8/13. Attack the weaker opponent and try always to win, for certain, your own service game. Finally, remember, if your opponents are at the net, hit very low, or very, very, high; if in doubt at all hit hard and low down the middle and if you stand in the same place twice you are bound to be wrong!

(Note: The chart on pages 112-113 will help further your understanding of on court moves; it describes seconds on court, it provides a few minutes reading, but go out and experiment for hours; you practise for years in order to be able to react effectively in less than a fifth of a second!)

8/13 Doubles tactics are aimed at command of the net

In Figure 6/2 back in Chapter 6 on Volley, you will have seen how server moved in to join partner near the net. The receiving pair must try to do exactly the same. In the illustration on the right here, **YOU (Y)** are the receiver. Your partner **(YP)** will stand, covering the other half of the court, just inside the service-line, or, if the opponent's serving is very severe on fast courts, back level with you on the baseline in the defensive position **(YPD)**.

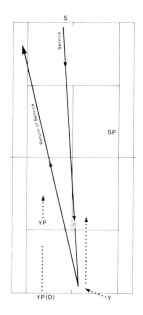

You **(Y)** should attempt to return service to keep server back, or to make server volley awkwardly, whilst you edge in towards net, or race there if your return is good!

Obviously, the exact pattern will depend a little on your standard and your opponent's standard, also. on where your opponents actually are positioned on the court. Your return, too, should occasionally vary with a lob over server's partner, or a drive down the tramlines and even the score will have an effect on what you do!

However, in the end in doubles, it comes down to two people trying to cover three 'gaps'. In the illustrations below, the ball from **your** previous shot has been played at the point 'O' and the gaps your opponents might aim for are denoted by the three long arrows. You **(Y)** and your partner **(YP)** must endeavour to close up the two 'gaps' that are easiest for your opponents to exploit and take the risk of leaving temporarily unguarded the space into which it is difficult for them to place the ball.

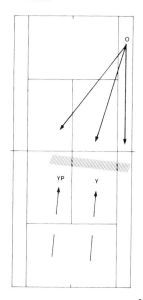
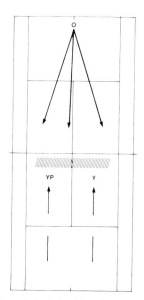
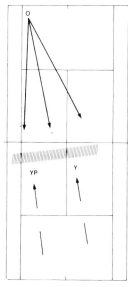

Never forget that doubles is a team game.
Either player of the pair standing in the same place twice   is certain to be wrong!
(Either the first time, or the second time!)

8/14 The One-Two Trick

When an opponent is at the net (especially in Singles) do not necessarily risk an error by trying an immediate passing shot off a difficult ball. Attempt to pull him out of position with a well directed shot **ONE** and then pass into the space **TWO**.

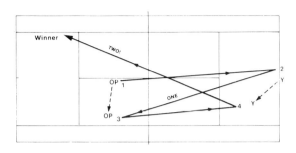

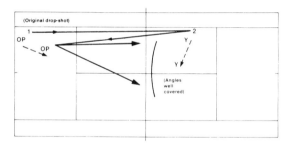

8/15 Get it straight!

If you are drawn in by a reasonably good drop-shot from your opponent, remember that unless you are attacking a known weakness, or unless you play a countering drop-shot, or hit a decisive cross-court winner, you should usually go straight down the line (forehand, or backhand) to narrow the angle of your opponent's next shot. Note, too, in case "you" are "the opponent" the next time, how he has moved in a little himself following his original drop-shot.

You and tennis

The second part of using your tennis brain covers:

(i) Becoming aware of the mechanisms within the game and within sport in any country.

(ii) Literally understanding the simple rules and later most of the commoner rules of the game.

(iii) Getting familiar with the main terms used.

The 'You and Tennis' model gives you an example of how you might move up through the various levels, either right to the top, or levelling out en route to enjoy tennis at a level you choose because it fits in with other interests and priorities in your life, or going as far as your sheer tennis ability will take you.

The model is based on the pattern of tennis in the United Kingdom, but the mechanism is similar in most countries.

Organisations

Each country has a national organisation – in Britain The Lawn Tennis Association (The LTA) which is affiliated to The International Tennis Federation (ITF).

In turn the LTA has affiliated to it, county LTA's, regional committees, and specialist groups such as umpires, referees and veterans, etc. An association such as The PTCA (The Professional Tennis Coaches' Association) although independent as the voice of coaches, would work closely with the LTA as the game's governing body and The LTA is in membership of The Central Council of Physical Recreation, which is a voice for all sports nationally. The Sports Council's finance and staff assist The LTA in the development of tennis. Also, of course, schools, colleges, local authorities, etc, all provide courts; as do over two thousand tennis clubs. If you enjoy your first few sessions of tennis, perhaps orginally at school, or in the park with a friend, or relative, or at an LTA open-centre, your next step really is to join your nearest club. Probably one of the staff at school would advise you whom to contact, or, enquire at the local library, etc. You could certainly write to: The LTA, Barons Court, West Kensington, London W14, who would gladly give you your county secretary's address and phone number for you to follow up a club membership enquiry with them. The LTA would also give you a contact for coaching opportunities, or you could write direct to: The Professional Tennis Coaches' Association, 21, Glencairn Court, Lansdown Road, Cheltenham, Gloucestershire, GL50 2NB. All countries have a national (and local LTA), so if you are reading this book outside Britain, it should be very easy to get the necessary details, but if not write to: The ITF, Barons Court, West Kensington, London W14, Great Britain.

Rules and Terms

The essential movement and competition of tennis may certainly be thoroughly enjoyed with only the simplest knowledge of the rules; use any form of scoring you like; even dispense with service at first, but, obviously, only play within the proper rules will give the fullest enjoyment and satisfaction. *The Rules of Tennis* booklet, simply explaining the rules as well as listing them in full, is obtainable from The LTA, but your own observation locally and of television matches and questions to more experienced players, will soon give you an adequate working knowledge of both the rules and the main terms. The history of tennis is fascinating too, descending from a game of hand and ball played over hedges in the fields, a little like modern volleyball, and then played with rackets in monasteries and big houses of France in the Middle Ages, only coming out on to the 'lawn' in the early 1870's and being called lawn tennis. Lord Aberdare's book, *The History of Tennis,* is well worth reading.

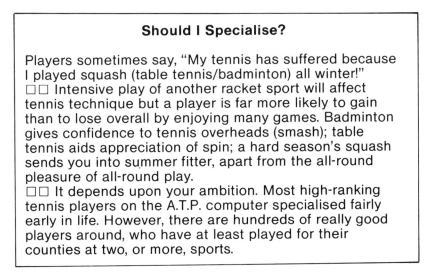

Should I Specialise?

Players sometimes say, "My tennis has suffered because I played squash (table tennis/badminton) all winter!" □□ Intensive play of another racket sport will affect tennis technique but a player is far more likely to gain than to lose overall by enjoying many games. Badminton gives confidence to tennis overheads (smash); table tennis aids appreciation of spin; a hard season's squash sends you into summer fitter, apart from the all-round pleasure of all-round play. □□ It depends upon your ambition. Most high-ranking tennis players on the A.T.P. computer specialised fairly early in life. However, there are hundreds of really good players around, who have at least played for their counties at two, or more, sports.

You In Action On Court
Information Centres

BALL	BAT	BODY		BRAIN	
Time Scale	Racket Hand	Body's Position	Eyes and Ears	Memory	Decisions to be made
You hit the ball	Feel of shot, length, speed, direction, spin is relayed to your brain.	Your body if unbalanced recovers, and gets itself ready for the brain's next command	Your eyes follow the ball and note also your opponent's initial reaction	Brain reminds you that last time in this situation you were too slow getting weight back over both feet and turning!	Get back from the extreme side of court where opponent's shot has forced you
Ball is nearly bouncing on opponent's side	Racket gripped loosely but not impeding body's movement	Your legs feel tired but move you towards centre of your baseline, slowly	Is your shot dropping short or is it still pushing opponent back; read opponent's body – does a fast heavy shot look likely, or a slow one, or an angle?	Slowly because memory tells you that last time you rushed across and opponent hit to just where you had been!	Does it look likely that your shot will cause opponent problems, or will he attack you strongly from a good position? Edge back, from or forward of baseline and therefore these decisions to be made
Ball bounces and quite sharply	Racket still comfortably ready	Your body reports that it is well balanced just behind centre of baseline	It looks as if opponent will have a problem picking up such a shooter, but his racket head is moving very fast	Last time this shooter happened, the opponent's shot bounced weakly mid-court for you	Take a chance and move forward ready to sweep weak shot back to opponent and perhaps follow up to net
Opponent strikes ball	Racket hand feels for appropriate grip	Body is too far forward; weight must be pulled back, turn must be started and a course set at an angle to ball's flight to get well back from its bounce	Eyes tell you that opponent has risked all and has hit very fiercely from low down, has aimed just to clear net, and ball looking to be going very wide to your backhand side. Ears tell you that opponent's strings scraped ball but still seemed to hit fairly fully and heavily	Brain reminds you that racket face of opponent was open, ball is going long but flight is slowish and back-spin is almost certainly on ball	Decision made to go well back and meet the ball rather than cut it off and brain also alerted that a defensive decision is likely
Ball is about to bounce your side	Racket is held in backhand grip and is already well back in preparation	Legs spring and work a little faster, you have further to go, body's balancing mechanisms prepare themselves for a last second long stretch of leading leg.	Eyes glued to ball, inform you that it's travelling faster than you thought and really spinning also. Its just a little wider in angle than you first perceived	Brain flashes up a message, last time the racket needed to be brought through very quickly and held very firm on this shot and stretch nearly took you off balance	Definitely a safe backhand return must be played, no chance of a winner this time, but which direction?

Ball is just about to be hit by you	Racket grip is firm; hand reports to brain that face is starting at the correct angle but messages take so long between hand and brain, we must hope for the best from now on in this stroke!	Body is well balanced, knees have bent, foot slid a little more than anticipated but racket-hand can cope with that alteration	Ball did skid off ground but you spotted it and message got through to get racket lower and more open; eyes distant spies also tell you opponent has not come to the net	Brain urges stay with follow-through for that extra bit of length that will be so useful for limiting opponent's next attack!	Back to opponent's backhand; or down line. We are balanced, no real panic, so back to his backhand if possible.
Ball is hit	Racket felt firm in hand, ball was controlled, and sheer weight and length of shot noted and passed to memory for storage; too late to help this shot but useful later	Body staying steady in follow through and trying to carry out brain's command to ease it inch by inch further to opponent's backhand	Eyes still telling you that ball is quick on and off racket and starting to pick up direction of your shot and opponent's reaction.	Brain is considering where was opponent and where might he move and what response both he and you made last time in this situation	Recovery back to centre, or possibly has it been a good enough shot to follow-up to net
Ball is en route well across to opponent's backhand	Racket hand relaxes and left hand helps take weight as position normalises	Body reports that it is ready to follow-up to net, or return a little towards centre of baseline.	Eyes note severity of shot and that opponent's body looks to be defensively poised, back a little not aggressively forward	Brain remembers advice that a cross-court follow-up is risky and also recalls what a fierce backhand opponent has just played.	Decision is made not to run to net but to be ready to pounce on opponent's next stroke if it should be a little weak

(and so on!)

(Think about it!)

113

YOU AND TENNIS AT ASCENDING LEVELS
Start at foot of page, left hand side and follow the appropriate arrows and boxes

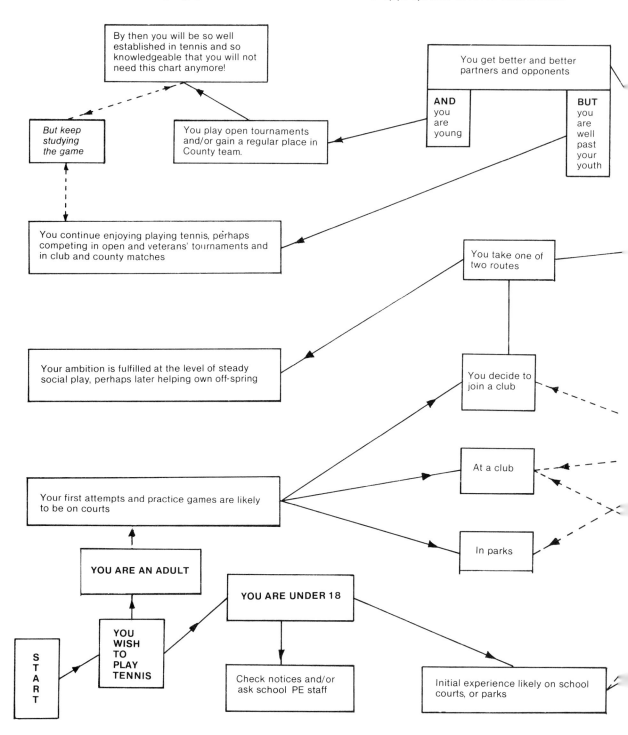

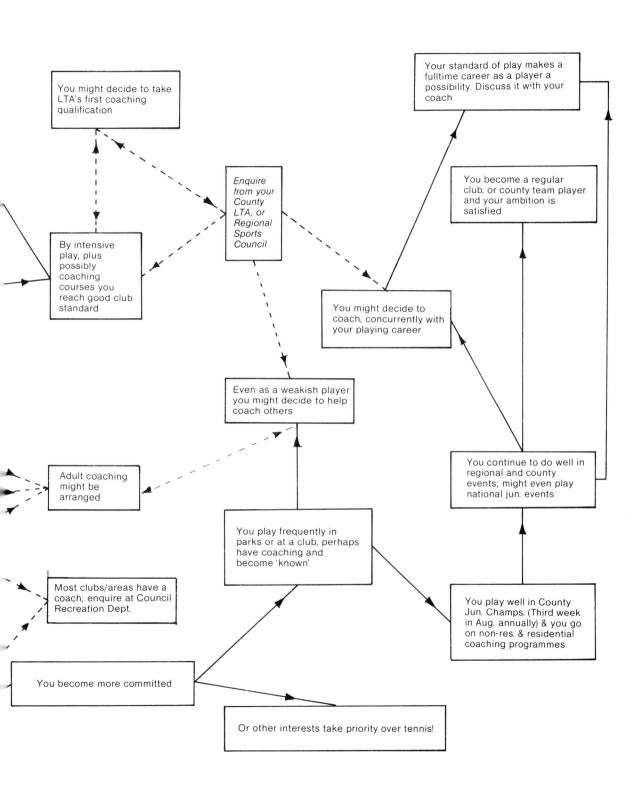

You might decide to take LTA's first coaching qualification

Your standard of play makes a fulltime career as a player a possibility. Discuss it with your coach

Enquire from your County LTA, or Regional Sports Council

You become a regular club, or county team player and your ambition is satisfied

By intensive play, plus possibly coaching courses you reach good club standard

You might decide to coach, concurrently with your playing career

Even as a weakish player you might decide to help coach others

You continue to do well in regional and county events; might even play national jun. events

Adult coaching might be arranged

You play frequently in parks or at a club, perhaps have coaching and become 'known'

Most clubs/areas have a coach; enquire at Council Recreation Dept.

You play well in County Jun. Champs. (Third week in Aug. annually) & you go on non-res. & residential coaching programmes

You become more committed

Or other interests take priority over tennis!

'MECHANISMS' WITHIN TENNIS (*Likely to be helpful to, and important in, your personal progress*)

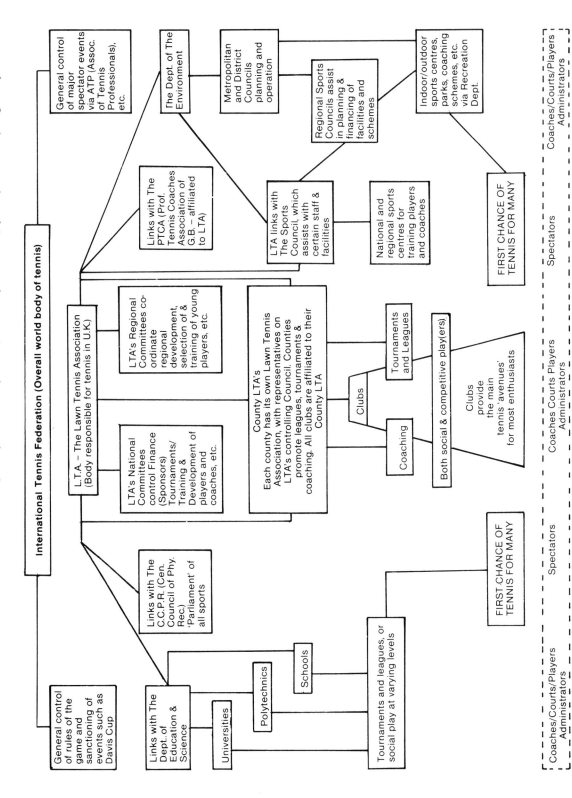

International Tennis Federation (Overall world body of tennis)

General control of major spectator events via ATP (Assoc. of Tennis Professionals), etc.

General control of rules of the game and sanctioning of events such as Davis Cup

The Dept. of The Environment

Metropolitan and District Councils planning and operation

Regional Sports Councils assist in planning & financing of facilities and schemes

Indoor/outdoor sports centres, parks, coaching schemes, etc. via Recreation Dept.

Links with The PTCA (Prof. Tennis Coaches Association of G.B. – affiliated to LTA)

LTA links with The Sports Council, which assists with certain staff & facilities

National and regional sports centres for training players and coaches

FIRST CHANCE OF TENNIS FOR MANY

L.T.A. – The Lawn Tennis Association (Body responsible for tennis in U.K.)

LTA's Regional Committees co-ordinate regional development, selection of & training of young players, etc.

LTA's National Committees control Finance (Sponsors) Tournaments/ Training & Development of players and coaches, etc.

County LTA's
Each county has its own Lawn Tennis Association, with representatives on LTA's controlling Council. Counties promote leagues, tournaments & coaching. All clubs are affiliated to their County LTA

Tournaments and Leagues

Clubs

Coaching

Clubs provide the main tennis 'avenues' for most enthusiasts

Both social & competitive player(s)

Links with The C.C.P.R. (Cen. Council of Phy. Rec.) 'Parliament' of all sports

Links with The Dept. of Education & Science

Universities

Polytechnics

Schools

Tournaments and leagues, or social play at varying levels

FIRST CHANCE OF TENNIS FOR MANY

Coaches/Courts/Players Administrators

Spectators

Coaches/Courts/Players Administrators

Coaches Courts Players Administrators

Spectators

Coaches/Courts/Players Administrators

8/16 Note the ideal grip size of racket in the hand of Jo Louis (1982 British Junior Champion). There is just a slight gap (½ in) between the base of the thumb and the tip of the fourth finger. (The thumb of your free hand should just be able to squeeze edge-on between the tip of that fourth-finger of your racket-hand and the base of the thumb of your racket-hand). (Also, can you read the 'signals', too? The position of BALL, BAT (racket) and BODY tell you that Jo's BRAIN has decided to attack this low ball with top-spin).

Jo favours a larger racket head and these Midi and Maxi sizes are now suitably available for most ages, but the Racket-selection-chart (page 104) indicates lighter normal-headed-rackets for most younger juniors, as service and volley techniques tend to develop better with these. Current trends, even with 'larger men' are towards lighter, thinner gripped, but larger headed, rackets.

9. BALL/BAT/BODY/BRAIN BLENDED

The four inescapable themes in this book have been

Ball   —   Bat   —   Body   —   Brain
     (Racket)

and, when examinining anything, it is useful to have such easily remembered headings.

However, it is the total blend that is ultimately important. Glib phrases abound in the world about, "Getting it all together; playing the music not the notes; the sum of the parts being greater than the whole," and your approach to tennis needs such a unity of understanding and purpose.

UNDERSTANDING

At whatever age you are reading this book, it will have failed, if you have not throuroughly understood the advice given. It has been aimed at a reasonably literate, but inexperienced, tennis hopeful, with at least a moderate interest in making on-court progress. If youthful, the progress could be very marked and even if elderly the decline in prowess might be arrested for a while! The volume should also be of value to more advanced players and particularly to such players who have an interest in coaching, or wish to guide sons/daughters/nephews/nieces/young friends, etc.

If a reader finds certain sections difficult, examine them again, especially after on-court experiment. In such difficulties find a 'wiser' friend (not necessarily a stronger tennis player!) to explore the tough passages with you.

Every subject has a code of 'key-words' that helps the process of understanding that subject. A code of vital terms that unlocks the mysteries, if the key-words themselves are unlocked first. Tennis is no exception. One does not have to be scholarly to be a great tennis player, but spend a few minutes glancing at the list below and try to define these terms, so important in understanding real progress in tennis.

Often players and even commentators and coaches use these terms very loosely and confusingly. Can you be more scientific and precise? Again, it will be the real competitors who accept the challenge of testing themselves before turning overleaf to check out these terms!

Ball-sense	Performance	Style
(A) Coach	Skill	Tactics
Learning	Strategy	Technique

Understanding the main terms

Check overleaf and see how near were your definitions to these. Remember, language generates its own change and words used in one 'register' have different meanings from their use in another (e.g., the word LET means four entirely different things to tennis players/estate agents/scientists/lawyers!).

Above the words were listed alphabetically, but here they are linked progressively in direct application to a tennis player's understanding and purpose.

Learning   is a permanent (or near permanent) change in the way a player responds to the same stimulus, (e.g., if a player modifies his/her backhand grip and, no matter what the pressure and situation, regularly hits successful backhands with the new grip, he/she could be said to have learned the new response); learning is not the absorption of facts and guidelines – it is how these modify the response; learning cannot really be accurately measured, but 'performance' is a good indicator; remember learning can be negative too – i.e., you could 'learn' to do something *less* effectively than before!

Performance in tennis, is to carry your strategical and tactical intentions into effect on court; performance is affected by internal and external motivation and by other factors, such as the general environment (under pressure, or relaxed) and your own state (whether fresh, or tired).

(A) Coach helps to reduce, with appropriate speed, the gap between what a player actually achieves and what he/she is capable of achieving.

Ball-sense is the ability to react effectively to a moving ball; everyone will have very well/well/poorly or very poorly/developed ball-sense, depending on nature's good fortune (inherited) and early experience (nurture); some will have a 'natural' reaction time faster than others and nothing can alter this, but the time it takes for an effective tactical *'choice'* to be made by your tennis brain can be so reduced by intelligent practice that even those with initially slow reactions and poor ball-sense can become really good competitive players.

Technique is 'a' method of performance – there is no such thing as 'the' method of performance; a coach attempts to ensure that the player's method of performance is effective in a majority of situations.

Skill   is the result of a player's (and a coach's) efforts welding Technique + Timing + Tactics
(i.e. Skill = Technique plus Timing plus Tactics);
skill is an efficient technique, readily performable and suited to the tactical decision.

Strategy   is the overall planning of your tennis future (grand strategy), or your preparations for a particular match and your overall plan for, and during, a match.

Tactics   are your moves and counter-moves on court aimed at beating your opponent(s) in each developing situation.

Style   is a personal way of expressing yourself in tennis play, via the way you perform tennis techniques and the tactics you adopt.

If you are very young, ask an adult to go through these definitions with you.

Whatever age you are, do not attempt to memorise all these meanings, unless the sheer mental exercise attracts you, or you have serious coaching aspirations. Just let this knowledge influence *your* understanding of *your* approach to tennis, which must in the end be personally satisfying and pleasing to you and you alone. Let it be 'your' style.

Style is the personal way you express yourself in your play. Let us take the 'p' out of 'personal' and the 'p' of 'play' and see what are the four main influences on a 'person's' style.

Personality — Physique — Place — Period

Personality Your personality will influence the way that you play. Often an adventurous and confident person will be a bold attacker on court and a

121

more cautious individual will operate carefully and defensively. Sometimes a person's on-court approach will differ markedly from their normal social manner and it could be that, through games, the real self is displayed. Certain players will clothe their technique with an especially pleasing and smooth way of executing strokes and will move with rhythm and grace. They will often be termed 'stylish players'. Nevertheless, the person who prefers purely functional strokes, with no thought of elegance, is also expressing their personal 'style'.

Physique Obviously a tall, heavily built, person will stroke the ball in a different way from a short, thin person. If the heavier person is really heavy and cumbersome and the small one is highly athletic and fast, then each one's tactics will also be conditioned partially by their physique. If a favourite player of yours has a totally different physique from you, he/she might still influence the way you play, but the way you are built will always show through in your overall game.

Place Where you were born, where you live, where you play and with whom and against whom you play, are all likely to influence the way you play. An African, with generations of his/her family having lived in an equatorial climate, will have a looser muscle structure, being 'naturally' supple, whereas a player from an old family in Northern Sweden would probably have a thicker muscle viscosity. Someone who learnt their tennis on the fast grass of South Africa, or on Californian courts, would develop differently from a player who spent their formative tennis years in Hungary and so on. The best player(s) in your school/club could well influence your own style, as could a coach, or a parent's way of playing.

Period The years during which you learn tennis influence the way you play. Just as the style in which music is composed and played, poetry read, buildings designed, paintings created, clothes worn and cars manufactured, changes from period to period, so does the way tennis is played.

Your parents and usually your coach and/or the senior players in your main teams, will all almost certainly have developed their game much earlier than you. Therefore, they should not try to impose their 'style' on you and you should not feel uneasy if your way of playing is markedly different. Follow such players' guidance and the advice of this book on the broad 'technical' principles, on which most agree

- good relationship to the ball (BALL)
- effective use of the racket-head (BAT)
- control of footwork and balance (BODY)
- sensibe and logical tactics (BRAIN)

and let the 'style' of performance be your very own.

Are you on the way **'UP'**?

(i.e., are you **U**nderstanding your personal approach and your **P**urpose on court?)

PURPOSE

You have almost certainly given this some thought already and these points will have occurred to you.

Tennis is played because
- it is fun
- it is (usually!) healthy
- it is a medium for meeting people
- it is challenging mentally and physically
- it is satisfying just hitting and controlling a ball, even if most points are lost.

Consequently, the two main reasons for being on court at all, singles or doubles, are –

to win and **to enjoy the process of winning**

Winning is far more enjoyable than losing, so plan to win – do not just plan to win – **plan** to win!

The factors in winning performances are these –

Prowess   – your prowess (skill) in match situations
Logic   – your logical approach to tactics
Ammunition   – your physical and mental fitness for the task in hand –
                          your speed, strength, suppleness and stamina and your
                          motivation, courage and determination
Next objective– your overall strategy and purpose.

Earlier chapters have, it is hoped, highlighted vital points for attention in all these areas, but a major summing-up of a player's detailed **purpose** on and off court might be helpful.

In **singles** your **purpose** is

1. To ensure that the ball is returned effectively.
2. To be certain that after ensuring that return you immediately move to the best possible position for the next anticipated shot, if there is one.
3. To try to bring your best shots to bear on your opponent's weakest ones.
4. To force your opponent to meet the ball in parts of the court that you dictate.
5. To deceive your opponent by surprising changes of length, angle, speed and spin.
6. To suit your overall approach to the score, the conditions, and the surface.
7. To act as well as react.

This would be a reasonable order of singles' priorities and one vital piece of simple advice fits in with every one of these principles –

never be *more* than 80 feet from your opponent and aim often to be much, much nearer.

The court is 78 feet long and, by the very nature and laws of service and return, you are likely to start about 80 feet from your opponent. So, if a shot of yours takes your opponent wide and/or deep in his/her own court, edge towards him/her, maintaining or even, decreasing that 80 feet gap. You will always have time to recover back a few feet before a ball travels that 80 feet towards your court and if your opponent is in real trouble you will be poised

124

to take advantage of the situation – maybe even moving right into the net, so that only 40, or 50 feet, seperate you both. Similarly, if your opponent has an easy smash at the net (opponent standing about 10 feet away from net) and you are inside your baseline, you are about 50 feet from him, or her, so widen the gap by back-pedalling quickly. In this instance, you would hit the surround-netting before you put 80 feet between you, but unless you are already tournament-class, those urgent few paces backwards will increase your chances of returning an attempted 'kill' by your opponent.

Remember that 'never-more-than-80-feet' tip next time you go on court.

In **doubles** your **purpose** is

1. To ensure that the ball is returned effectively.
2. To be certain that after ensuring such return you and your partner move to be level with each other across the court – dominating the net if possible; defending wide and deep on baseline if not possible, or, providing you are *level across the court,* even in 'no-mans-land'. (See illustration 8/13) (If you aim to play good doubles you must recognise that one player at the net and one at the baseline is as bad as a double-fault on service!)
3. To be determined 'to get and keep together' by limiting the time and space that you are apart, if you and your partner are temporarily separated by the situation (such as service and return of service, or one player forced out of position). Frequent casual loss of this vital 'level' alignment on court is a recipe for disaster.
4. To try and play shots (including well directed first services and returns of service) that are likely to 'involve' your partner – setting up good attacking opportunities for partner, or limiting partner's 'exposure'.
5. To be ruthless in always placing the ball more towards the weaker, more exposed, or more unbalanced, opponent.
6. To endeavour, when your opponents are at the net, to keep the ball low (even if slow!), or to put it very high indeed; if in doubt direct your shot down the middle.

7. To exploit your partner's strengths and cover up their weaknesses.

If you both keep these principles in mind, then you really are a doubles team and not just two singles players who happen to be on the same side of the net as each other.

Problems

Any good general will always examine in advance possible snags that might upset the plan of campaign. Such a commander will, of course, have considerable assistance from staff officers and other specialists and account will have to be taken of numerous matters not directly connected with the 'battle'. You are not alone in your tennis at any level, although, often in a tough singles-match, your side of the net can seem a very lonely place. Frequently, team-mates will be a part of your tennis scene but scores of other people are directly and indirectly concerned, too.

Look at page 132 and see who and what is involved in 'your' tennis. Even if you are a young junior in your first season in the game and first week at the club, others are essential to what is happening. Your parents probably encouraged you and purchased vital equipment; the club secretary oversees things and there is probably a professional, or voluntary, club coach to help everyone. Should you be an adult who wishes to enjoy the weekly game in high summer in the local parks, there has to be a park-keeper, plus a groundsman, council officials, who planned the courts, and councillors who vote the funds for the upkeep, etc.

Failure to recognise and appreciate who is important in your tennis development could in itself be a snag, but there are other potential problems that need to be identified. Successfully spotlighting likely snags is always the first step to eliminating them as problems.

Obviously, if your ambition and interest in tennis is of very modest proportions, then these problems will be proportionally of little worry, or importance, but assuming a fairly strong urge for enjoyable success in the game, adult or junior, consider the next few pages and relate and expand to fit your situation.

1. **Travel** – long distance travel, especially by air and to a playing venue different in altitude from your normal abode, requires a period of acclimatisation, before peak performance is likely. Rarely will readers of this book be in extreme situations – a match on the other side of the world and a change of thousands of feet in altitude – but quite likely a player will move from an inland northern city to a south-coast seaside resort. What a pity it would be to waste months of preparation by racing down motorways, arriving in the early hours and listlessly losing your first match! Ideally aim for a full day's acclimatisation before commencing any week-long campaign and, when driving over to those tough rivals for an evening match that could decide the local league, allow for a reasonable rest before serving that first ace! On any journey longer than an hour, make certain that you get out of any seat (plane, coach, train or car) and MOVE ABOUT.

2. **Sleep** – is one of the four main factors in any preparation for physical performance; appropriate exercise, nutrition and environment are the others. If you have an important match on the morrow try to keep the pre-match hours as normal as possible. If, for example, you always go to bed at, or after 1 a.m., having been to a disco, the pub, or the social club, then drawing the curtains and retiring at 9 p.m. could well mean a long, disturbed night! Physiologically there is no reason why a player, deprived of sleep for all of one night, should not perform remarkably well on court, although psychologically the player might 'feel' tired. Occasionally an outstanding performance will occur in such circumstances, very probably because the player has a ready-made excuse for losing and, therefore, not 'fearing' failure, actually succeeds. A player staggering off court having lost a close four-hour singles match might well feel that the steps up to the pavilion are too much for his/her exhausted state. However, should a bull suddenly appear in the gateway, the body would soon show that it had enormous reserves of fuel still left to power further fast movement.

127

Nevertheless a good night's sleep before an important match and a level of fitness that allows the match to be completed without apparent total exhaustion is desirable. So, if away, try to ensure sleeping arrangements similar to home and keep to normal habits.

3. **Nutrition** – within reason eat what you like and what suits you, remembering that an overweight player is unlikely to be as nippy about a court as a lean-greyhound. Protein, fats and carbohydrates are the vital body-fuels, with carbohydrates definitely being the prime energy source for high intensity exercise. Keep your pre-match diet as near as possible to your regular eating habits, but ensure that it includes a good carbohydrate percentage. 'Fast foods' do not automatically mean a 'fast player'. What is wanted is food that contains significant amounts of carbohydrates and protein, plus natural vitamins, for example, muesli, fruit and specially prepared 'Energy Bars'. Tuck-into the cereals, toast and honey, at breakfast. In the nervous tension before a match, eating and drinking might be uninviting. In a longish tournament, the interval between matches might again seem appropriate only for a fizzy-drink. A player should recognise these two periods of time as potential danger zones – problem areas. If a part of your tennis enjoyment is the consumption of alcohol, so be it, consume it and skip the next few lines. However, if you wish seriously to give of your physical and mental best, in matches, one after another, after another, then take note.

   (i) It would be wise to drink more than you feel you need before a match, choosing one of the electrolyte drinks that are now widely marketed. These are pleasant to take, have no side-effects and build up a vital water reserve for the inevitable sweat-loss. Even a small percentage loss of body-fluid diminishes performance, so build up that reserve and keep it topped up, whilst playing, by continuing to sip a suitable electrolyte drink – Mineral Plus 6 and XL1 are examples of leading drinks on the UK market, with Energy Drink for pre-match consumption.

(ii) Avoid unsuitable snacks during tournaments (chips/crisps/cakes/ peanuts/etc) and if the thought of a pre-match meal is distasteful, take a glass of a product such as Plus Food, containing, in a chocolate flavoured drink-form, all that is needed in place of a meal – high grade protein, vitamins, minerals and those carbohydrates again.

(iii) If a meal is preferred and suitably available, try to complete it about two hours before the match.

(iv) Avoid (especialy abroad and very especially in hot and/or underdeveloped lands) doubtful drinking water, iced-drinks and ice-cream and items that appear to have been in "show-cases" for long periods. Do not eat unwashed fruit, or vegetables, and leave any experiments with exotic local foods until after the finals. Take bottled water, or mineral water, with you.

(v) Do not take glucose just before a match and only take iron and/or vitamin pills with expert medical advice.

4. **Exercise** – obviously the main exercise for a tennis player is tennis itself and once a good basic level of fitness has been achieved (see page 105), intensive work on court is the answer. It is highly likely that if a tennis player devoted hours and hours each week to dedicated strength, speed and stamina training and kept supple, then overall their performance would improve on court. However, even most of the very top players do not view tennis this way and most readers of this book will be similarly minded. The training mentioned on page 105 (especially the running) is likely to be done by many readers and to the benefit of their tennis, but had they wished to spend long hours with weights, or at a track, they would probably have taken up weight-lifting, or athletics, as desirable activities in themselves. So – as a tennis player primarily and not an athlete, or weight-lifter – remember –

(i) Warm-up thoroughly before exercise and/or play and also

'warm-down'. Try not to get straight into your car and drive twenty-miles immediately after match-point.

(ii) Keep track-suits on until warm. Stretch and flex vital muscle groups.

(iii) Escalate gently by day, by week, by month, by season.

(iv) Pain is a warning – some, but only some, injuries are helped by exercise through the pain, but if it's painful when you move it, seriously consider stopping; if it's painful when someone else moves it, definitely stop! This can only be a very broad guide but with any injury seek a doctor's, or physiotherapist's, advice early on, do not soldier on!

5. **Environment** – is often very different for an important match. The player moves to, and is immediately highly active in, a different country or different locale, or plays suddenly in a hot oppressive, spectator surrounded bowl. Maybe, too, the player is temporarily living in a caravan. Such changes will influence food and drink intake habits and requirements, so do read the nutrition section carefully. A close confidant/supporter/relative, or other person encountered, might have obvious flu', or a cold, or a troubled tummy if abroad, so risk embarrassment, even arrogance, by avoiding their company – why waste a year's build up by a cold developing on the day of a final? If they really support you and your tennis success is important to both, they will understand.

Advice

The aim of these last few pages is not to take the joy out of your tennis play and travel, but exactly the opposite; the aim is to minimise the risks of tennis disappointment due to matters distant from an actual tennis court. Sport is now so much a part of UK life that experts, or reasonably informed people of sense and goodwill, are available for you to seek their advice

– your doctor, or a local physiotherapist, with a particular sporting interest

- your coach (and/or P.E. staff if you are still at school)
- your librarian (the local library will almost certainly have a volume on sports injuries and on diet for sport)
- your chemist (will almost certainly stock Energy Bars and electrolyte drinks – if not, order a small quantity from him)
- players in your locality who have experience of higher level play.

It is hoped that all this wide-ranging advice has been helpful to you in defining and achieving your own personal tennis purpose and the analysis on page 132 groups together who and what is involved at varying stages of tennis progress.

Finally, when you walk on court for that big match, remember that,
- if you are not 'nervous'
- if your legs do not feel like jelly
- and if your heart is not pounding,

then the match probably does not mean all that much to you. It is temporary over-motivation that is giving you these sensations and they will pass as the battle develops. In fact the fitter and more mentally prepared you are for the fray, the more noticeably and earlier might occur the sweaty palm and the beating heart. Every player in the world who really wants to win will experience what you do and 'experience' is just that,

– FIRST HAND KNOWLEDGE OF
WHAT IS ACTUALLY HAPPENING.

Look at the Who and What and When analysis on the next page and realise what 'support' there is all around you for enjoyable and successful tennis.

WHO and WHAT and WHEN?
As a player's tennis develops more and more is 'involved'

AGE and STANDARD	PEOPLE	DEVELOPMENTS	MECHANISMS and AGENCIES	FACILITIES and OTHER FACTORS
School-age participation	Family and friends School teaching staff (especially PE staff) 'Elementary' coaches If in a tennis-club, other club members	Early technical training Emergence of own style First steps competitively Probably commencement of 'spectator' interest watching TV, and/or local matches	Sports Council (Central Government aid to sport) Local Education Authority District/County Council Governing-body of tennis (LTA – club availability)	School courts, parks, and possibly club courts. Equipment and clothing purchased by parents, or rackets 'loaned' (See note – RACKETS)
Social adult play at modest performance levels	Family and friends Elementary coaches, locally and possibly tennis club members	Social contact; technical mastery; own style, maybe some competition; coach own children	Sports Council District/County Council LTA (indirectly) Firm's social/sports club	Parks and/or club courts Equipment purchased, hired or loaned; clothing purchased Spectator interest
Keen and fairly successful junior (U/18) player	Family and friends (for travel help especially) School staff Higher level coaches Honorary tennis administrators	More intensive coaching and training sessions Regular competitive play local and elsewhere	County LTA Sports Council County/District Council Education Authority (LEA) County junior 'squad'	More specialised equipment and sophisticated clothing; transport Club/indoor/county tennis centre courts. Financial assistance for coaching
Promising 'regionally-selected' junior (U/18)	Family and friends Full-time professional coaches and LTA's Regional Coach and administrative staff Journalists and commentators	Serious training daily Regular residential and non-residential training and coaching sessions Individual coaching; more sophisticated techniques; wider competition	The British Assoc. of National Coaches (BANC) PTCA (Prof. Tennis Coaches Association) The LEA/LTA Regional Committee District/County Council Regional junior 'squad'	Equipment and clothing provided free, or on concessionary terms National and regional tennis centre/clubs Coaching and competition grant-aided
Full-time, moderately successful player (Late teens/20's)	Family and friends (husband/wife). Fans. LTA staff, International Tennis Federation staff and personnel of other national LTA's Journalists, commentators, PR staff, sponsors' agents, personal agents Other full-time players/partners National team-mates	Tennis schedules govern social life, marriage plans, etc. National rankings, ATP computer points start to assume vital importance Wimbledon entry sought Frequent travel and hotel life-style	LTA's professional staff (Technical/administrative and financial) Association of Tennis Professionals (ATP) Sports Council TV channels Major sports goods manufacturers Tennis sponsors BANC/BASM/SSS (BAS & M = Brit. Assoc. of Sport & Medicine) (SSS = The Society of Sports Sciences)	Player becomes a 'model', copied by younger players both in style and behaviour International stadia Prize-money Fee income from 'endorsements' of rackets, clothing and other equipment and some non-tennis products
Top international tennis star	Family and friends Personal coach/manager. Fans. International officials. Journalists, commentators, PR staff, sponsors Fellow top competitors Celebrities and VIP's tennis and non-tennis	Prolonged exposure to public gaze Maybe special diet adopted High level medical and para-medical attention Investment of tennis and PR income (possibly into tennis-based initiative (coaching/facilities/equipment)	Security mechanisms, public and private International tennis bodies PR-firms & TV channels Financial and legal consultants BANC/BASM/SSS 'Jet-set' membership	Image and reputation become major PR asset for all types of commercial use Performance/statistics/etc become reference points and provide material for sports science future Appearances on TV and in coaching films, etc, influence rising tennis teenagers
After intensive playing life at top and other competitive levels is over	Family and friends Current competitors and ex-competitors Other acquaintances and contacts from playing years	Possible move into coaching/tennis commerce, or admin' Commentating/writing 'Putting something back into the game' Competing in 'senior' and 'veterans' events Possibly become a 'tennis politician', 'LTA councillor, etc.	ITF (Int. Tennis Fed.) LTA's (National & County) Sports Councils (National Regional and Local) TV. Tennis press, etc. CCPR (Central Council of Physical Recreation) Dept. of Environment, etc.	Maybe become a 'definitive reference' for the guidance of other players and coaches Possibly become the 'mentor' of (a) younger international tennis star(s)

Notes:
(i) **Rackets** – Care in choosing first and subsequent rackets is vital. Study racket-selection-chart on page 104 and take advice from your coach, especially. Look closely at the illustration 8/16 and note how to check the ideal grip size for you. Remember, lighter, thinner, rackets help speedier movements; heavier models give solid control and power. Larger head sizes allow more room for error. Wood and graphite (injection moulded) rackets absorb shock better than steel rackets. High tension stringing, especially natural gut, is only for champions, or real hopefuls; 56lbs/66lbs tension would be advisable for most, and man-made stringing materials last longer, especially in poor weather. Too much variation in rackets used and stringing tensions, particularly if combined with varying playing surfaces, increase the chances of tennis elbow, as does wrong grip size.

(ii) The main 'Sports Sciences' are – Sports Psychology – Exercise Physiology – Bio-Chemistry – Bio-Mechanics – Dietetics.

132

CONCLUSION

It is hoped that these few pages will have increased your knowledge of the game and how you actually want to play it and will have increased your desire to play it frequently and well.

Keep in mind the three stonemasons questioned on what they were doing.

One replied, 'Working with this piece of stone'.

The second said, 'Earning a penny a day and a bowl of soup';

and the third said, 'Helping Sir Christopher Wren to build a cathedral!'

Are you the first stonemason? Are you just knocking a ball about, or are you the second stonemason? Are you trying hard for the prize-money, the cup, working conscientiously because you, or with young players your parents, have paid for the lessons, or are you the third stonemason? If you are the third, the overall game means something to you, all your efforts are co-ordinated and tennis helps you to a fuller understanding of yourself and of your path through life.

'Remember you only know where you are, when you know where you have been!'

THE BEGINNING . . . . . .